# CHRISTIAN EDUCATION
## Issues of the Day

# CHRISTIAN EDUCATION
Issues of the Day

John B. Hulst

Dordt College Press

Cover by Rindy De Nooy
Layout by Carla Goslinga

Copyright © 2012 by John B. Hulst

Unless otherwise noted quotations from Scripture are taken from the NIV.
Scripture taken from the HOLY BIBLE, NEW INTERNATIONAL VERSION®. NIV®. Copyright © 1973, 1978, 1984 by International Bible Society. Used by permission of Zondervan Publishing House. All rights reserved.

Fragmentary portions of this book may be freely used by those who are interested in sharing the author's insights and observations, so long as the material is not pirated for monetary gain and so long as proper credit is visibly given to the publisher and the author. Others, and those who wish to use larger sections of text, must seek written permission from the publisher.

*Printed in the United States of America.*

Dordt College Press
498 Fourth Avenue NE
Sioux Center, Iowa 51250
United States of America

www.dordt.edu/dordt_press

ISBN: 978-0-932914-94-1

The Library of Congress Cataloging-in-Publication Data is on file with the Library of Congress, Washington, D.C.

Library of Congress Control Number: 2012940870

# Table of Contents

Prologue ........................................................................................ 1
1. A Place for Dordt College ................................................. 7
2. Christian World View and Scholarship ........................... 19
3. Education for the Kingdom of God:
   Christian Education in a Plural Society ......................... 43
4. The Relation between the Bible and Science .................. 63
5. Leadership in the Christian School ................................. 75
6. Creating a Community .................................................... 87
7. A View from the Christian School Classroom ................ 97
8. Teaching Bible in the Christian School ......................... 109
9. Educating for Stewardship ............................................. 127
10. Christian Education and Creativity ............................... 139
11. Preparing Christian Teachers for the Future ................. 153
12. Christian Education and the Future of the Kingdom ... 163
Epilogue ................................................................................... 173

# Prologue

During my 28 year tenure at Dordt College, I was privileged to be involved in the formulation and articulation of its Basis Statement and its Statement of Purpose, as well as its 1989 Strategic Plan, titled "Renewing Our Vision." During the same time, I was being invited to speak on "issues of the day" to Christian educational conferences and conventions, not only in the United States but throughout the world. These speeches, while concerned with Christian education on all levels, naturally and inevitably reflected the work I was doing with others regarding the perspective to be reflected in Dordt's academic program.

One occasion stands out in particular. In 1996 Kosin University, Busan, South Korea, celebrated its 50th Anniversary. Since we had just established an official relationship with Kosin, I was asked to represent Dordt at the celebration and to speak specifically on or about "The Educational Framework of Dordt College." (The speech given on that occasion is not included in this book because, while it illustrates the point being made, it was based entirely on a document produced by the faculty.) Dordt's Statement of Purpose mandates the faculty to the ongoing task of developing an integrated curriculum and to work together in developing strategies to foster interdisciplinary learning. The faculty, under the leadership of Dr. Rockne McCarthy, responded to this mandate by adopting the Educational Framework document, which clarifies what the curriculum should be and how it should be structured to fulfill the mission of the college. As the preface to the document indicates, it is not intended to be the final word but to be a contribution to the ongoing work of curricular reform. The positive response to the presentation at Kosin University indicated appreciation for Dordt's commitment to reformational learning.

That same year, 1996, was also the year I retired as the president of Dordt College. At my last meeting with the Board of Trustees I took the opportunity to thank the Board for giving me the opportunity to serve the cause of Christian higher education and to remind the Board of the importance of remaining true to its reformational perspective—a responsibility clearly set forth in the Statement of Purpose:

The board's specific task was . . . . to provide leadership, especially to guide the religious direction and to ensure its academic excellence.

Since that time there have been several occasions when I have wondered what I could do as president emeritus to encourage the College to continue to implant the principles enunciated in this statement.

One such occasion occurred in 1998 when Eerdmans published *The Dying of the Light* by James Tunstead Burtchaell. In this 868 page volume, according to the sub-title, the author points to "The Disengagement of Colleges and Universities from their Christian Churches" as the reason for "the dying of the light" of Christian belief in many of these institutions. The last college to be considered was Dordt College. I was shocked, as were others, to learn that Dordt was included as one of the colleges in which the "light" was dying. When I expressed my dismay to one of my colleagues from another college, he responded, "John, Burtchaell doesn't really understand Dordt College." I believe that's true, primarily because Burtchaell is viewing Dordt from a Thomistic perspective that holds that the "light" depends upon an official connection with the instituted church and its creeds, whereas Dordt emphasizes the need to fuel the "light" with an ongoing commitment to a biblical, Reformed, Christian academic perspective. In any case, this incident among others made me aware of the importance of supporting the College in maintaining its kingdom vision. But how?

After concluding six years of service as executive secretary of the International Association for the Promotion of Christian Higher Education (1996–2002), it was suggested that I commit some of my "free time" to publishing a number of the speeches given during and following my tenure at Dordt. My initial response was negative, in part because I knew how much work would be involved. Still, I began to realize that this could be one small way to support the "spiritual direction" and "academic excellence" of the College. Therefore, some time before we moved from Sioux Center to Pella, Iowa, I met to discuss the project with Dr. John Kok of Dordt Press and eventually decided to begin work on a twelve speech/chapter publication.

The purpose from the beginning has been to reflect my understanding of Dordt's reformational vision, not only in teacher education but in all of the disciplines. As you read through this brief volume you will notice frequent reference to the three basic biblical categories of creation, fall, and redemption. I trust this will not be regarded as needless, boring repetition. Instead it is intended to indicate that the sum of our reformational world view is this: 1) *creation* is much broader than we tend to think, 2) the *fall* affects the entire creation, and 3) *redemption* in Christ reaches as far as the fall.

A large part of my inspiration in all of this has been contact with Dordt alumni who are serving—many of them with distinction—in churches, education, finance, business, medicine, agriculture, government, communication, transportation, technology. Often they express gratitude for the quality of their college education and the kingdom vision they received while at Dordt. Just as often, those with whom and for whom they work will comment favorably on their ability, their work ethic, and their willingness to work in cooperation with others. This also explains why I frequently hear myself saying, "You know, don't you? He/she is a graduate of Dordt College."

For this reason I would like to *dedicate* this publication to the growing number of Dordt College alumni. Hopefully it reflects not only the integral Christian college education they received, but also the lives they are living. At the same time, I want to *thank* John Kok along with Sally Jongsma for their encouragement and editorial assistance, and my wife, Louise, for her constant loving support during the years of speaking and writing. Above all, I thank God for the opportunity to serve Him at Dordt in teaching, counseling, preaching, and speaking in promotion of His Kingdom.

J. B. Hulst

# Chapter One

**To the Reader –**

When I was a student at Calvin College in Grand Rapids, Michigan, (1947–1951), Calvin was the sole college of the Christian Reformed Church (CRC), owned and governed by the denomination. During these years there was some discussion about starting another CRC-related college in the Midwest, one that would likely be in competition with Calvin. Was there a legitimate place for such a college? Being a loyal student of Calvin College, my answer to the question was, "No, we don't need another college."

Some years later, when I graduated from Calvin Seminary and accepted a call to the Christian Reformed Church in Ireton, Iowa, I faced that question again. I was aware of the shortage of certified teachers for Christian schools—those who went to Calvin College to prepare for teaching tended to stay in Michigan rather than return to Iowa to teach—and I soon became convinced that there was a place for a Christian college with a teacher education program in the Midwest. In the beginning, teacher education was the primary focus of Dordt's program as a two-year college. But in a few years, the Board proposed expansion to a four-year liberal arts college with all subjects taught from a scripturally-oriented perspective. By this time, I was pastor of the First CRC in Orange City, Iowa, and joined with the Society in 1961 to promote the adoption of this proposed expansion.

But not everyone valued Dordt's place at the table. I recall serving as a representative of the Iowa Association of Independent Colleges and Universities on the advisory board of the Wallace Technology Foundation. The Foundation was established for the purpose of involving Iowa colleges and universities in the development of technology for the agricultural community. At one of the meetings, I spoke up on behalf of the Stewardship Center at Dordt College. A businessman responded in ridicule, stating that the board should not take seriously the viewpoint of "a small college in northwest Iowa"—implying that there really was no place for a college such as Dordt.

My tenure at Dordt College began in 1968. By 1982, when I was inaugurated as the second president of Dordt, I had been working at the college for fourteen years and had also spent a number of years on the Purposes Committee, involved in the writing and presentation of Dordt's purpose statement "The Educational Task of Dordt College." In 1981, I had earned the Th.D. in

Religion and Higher Education from the Iliff School of Theology in Denver Colorado. So, when the time came to deliver my inaugural address, I was not only convinced that there was a place for Dordt, but also felt prepared to present publicly the reasons why.

Thirty years later, now re-reading the inaugural address in preparation for publication, I believe that Dordt and similar colleges are still facing many of the same questions and challenges.

# A Place for Dordt College?

On March 18, 1982, I informed the Board of Trustees that I accepted their appointment to the presidency of Dordt College. I did so *gratefully*, realizing the honor involved; *hesitatingly*, aware of the demands of the position; *humbly*, conscious of personal limitations; but *confidently*, trusting in God's abiding presence and blessing. Also, I did so assuming that I would receive the support of the entire Dordt College community; not first of all for my sake, but for the sake of the college and the glory of its Lord. And since June 1, the time at which my work officially began, I have experienced that support.

**Challenges**

At the same time, I was and continue to be aware of the issues that challenge and even threaten an institution such as Dordt College.

Dordt is a *school*, an academic institution established for the purpose of providing formal education—primarily, but not solely, for young people. But presently schools are not being viewed with a great deal of appreciation. A recent *Time* article observes:

> Many of America's schools today teach precious little of what students ought to know, and that little ill. . . . Among educators there is a sense of desperation that America's young lack even the rudiments of learning, and a still greater feeling of despair that nothing can be done about it. (Stengel, 1982, p. 59)

This is hardly an encouraging note for those involved in formal education.

Further, Dordt is what is called a *liberal arts* school or college. As such, it is to be distinguished from schools described as "technical" or "vocational." But the future of colleges providing liberal education does not seem very promising. Just last year Theodore M. Hesburgh, well-known president of the University of Notre Dame, wrote:

> To question the future of liberal education, not only as it relates to the needs of a single campus but to the world at large as well, is no idle speculation. We seem to be passing through a time when education is

---

Inaugural address, 23 October 1982.

the more cherished as it is the more vocational; when learning how to *do* something, rather than . . . how to *be* someone, particularly someone human, is in vogue. Thus we must seriously address the future of liberal education. . . . (Hesburgh, 1981, p. 36)

Moreover, Dordt is known as a *private* college. As such it must be set apart from colleges and universities that are maintained almost solely by means of public funding, governed by public boards, and relatively open in terms of their admissions policies. And what are the predictions for private colleges? According to Fred Crossland, a program officer in the Education and Research Division of the Ford Foundation, "There is general agreement that the most endangered species are the public state colleges and the non-prestigious, tuition dependent private colleges and universities" (Crossland, 1980, pp. 22, 23). Mr. Crossland would probably view Dordt as a non-prestigious, tuition-dependent, private college.

Lest we suppose, however, that Mr. Crossland's prediction reflect a personally negative attitude toward private colleges, we must recognize that similar predictions are being made by statisticians in the confessional community from which Dordt draws the major part of its support and enrollment. Recently, a group meeting in Chicago, Illinois, was informed that enrollment projections are anything but bright for colleges, such as Dordt, that are associated with the Christian Reformed Church. Today there are approximately 4,500 Christian Reformed students in these schools. By 1990, if present trends and percentages continue, Christian Reformed students enrolled in these colleges could be down to 3,000 or 35 percent less than the present figure.

Finally, Dordt is characterized by many as a *Protestant evangelical* college. As Protestant, it is marked-off from Roman Catholic schools; and as evangelical it is distinguished from schools not concerned to base their programs on the evangelical Christian faith. And how is a Protestant evangelical school being viewed today? With appreciation by some, but certainly not by all.

In 1968 Christopher Jencks and David Riesman co-authored a book titled *The Academic Revolution*. In this work they describe with approval a development by means of which college and university faculties have increasingly gained hegemony over a large part of the academy. Freeing themselves from external controls, these faculties have engaged in research, built their departments, lessened student loads, and provided meaningful leadership in society. But there is one place in particular where this salutary development has not occurred. According to Riesman in a 1980 publication, *On Higher Education: The academic enterprise in an era of rising student consumerism,* there were all-along institutions not touched by the "academic revolution," or touched only marginally. Among these the most outstanding are the Protestant evangelical colleges. The implications are clear: in the eyes of such as Jencks and Riesman, while a Protestant evangelical college may be a safe and secure place for young people in their formative years, it certainly is not a place where one can expect to find academic leadership, progress, or excitement. For all of these we must look elsewhere.

As stated earlier, these issues seem to produce challenges that threaten the future of an institution such as Dordt College. Little stock is put in higher education per se; the trend is away from the kind of education that Dordt offers; predictions are that enrollments will decrease; and the academic work that Dordt is doing, because of its association with evangelical Christianity, has been termed insignificant. All of this together has caused some to ask: Is there a legitimate or necessary place in our society for a school, a college, such as Dordt College?

**A Conviction**

It should surprise no one that my answer to this question is an enthusiastically affirmative one. If it were not, I would have discouraged today's activities and would have done everything possible to avoid being placed in my present position. Yes, I do believe that there is a legitimate and necessary place in our society for an institution such as Dordt College.

But why, and on what grounds?

Do I hold this conviction because I have decided to ignore or reject the predictions? No; although I must admit that it was encouraging to read "The Future of Higher Education," an article by M. M. Chambers that appeared in a recent issue of *The Chronicle of Higher Education,* in which he writes that the predictions of impending disaster are "premature, to say the least, and probably wholly wrong" (Chambers, 1980, p. 72).

Do I have confidence in Dordt's future because I am aware of ways to meet the impending crisis? Not necessarily; although I did find it helpful to read in *Phi Delta Kappan* Ira Jay Winn's suggestion for three ways to deal with the enrollment crunch (Winn, 1980, pp. 686–87).

1. Open the doors wider to those who do not measure up to traditional standards.
2. Adjust the curriculum to meet current student interest.
3. Make available a meaningful program of continuing education.

Or is my belief that Dordt has a place in our society based upon a confidence in the future of democracy? Again, no; although I am pleased to know that there is a large number of people in our democratic society who share my conviction. They would argue their case in terms of pluralism—a pluralism which has in mind:

> ... the interaction of freely competing interest groups, often operating through lobbies, each exerting pressure upon the state in support of its private cause, with the state acting as an amoral power broker to maintain equilibrium among these many causes. (McCarthy, 1981, p. 31)

In this view our society must give place to colleges such as Dordt because they provide a way to balance educational budgets; they increase freedom of choice in education; they provide competition, which is healthy for both public and private colleges; and they diminish tensions in regard to differing school policies. Now I suppose that much of this is true, but this type of pluralism does not yet describe the reason for my conviction that there is a place in our society for Dordt College.

What, then, is the reason? I will begin to answer this question by acknowledging that I do indeed hold to a pluralistic view of society; but it is a pluralism that, because it acknowledges the sovereignty of God over all of life, is based on the thesis that "life is religion." Religion cannot be reduced to a small, limited, cultic segment of life. Religion is the very root of life. For, as Gordon Spykman observes, "... life in its total extent and in all its parts is a coherent complex of ongoing responses, obedient and disobedient, to God's claim on the whole man in all his life relationships" (1976, p. 165).

Do note, however, that the thesis that life is religion is not the result of an empirical analysis of reality. It is rather the fruit of a deep conviction based on God's revelation found in the infallible Scriptures of the Old and New Testaments. It is supported by the biblical teaching that our covenantal relationship with God embraces every walk of life as service before His face. It is rooted in the biblical view of the kingdom in which every task is a calling to live *pro rege*, i.e., for the King. Rejecting the notion of neutrality and believing that all human activity—including scientific activity—has a religious starting point, I wish now to share with you my personal conviction and, in the process, my academic confession of faith—a confession that, I trust, reflects that of the entire Dordt community.

According to the Scriptures, in the beginning God created the world in an orderly fashion—bringing into being His creation-kingdom. Doing so, He established the law that was to govern and structure the creation and gave to each part its own nature and task—making the world a cosmos rather than a chaos. God also created man in His image and called upon him to serve Him by developing the potentialities of creation according to God's law. The sum total of God's demand was that man, a kingdom citizen, lovingly serve God with all his heart—his heart being the concentration point of his entire existence. Thus, as Stuart Fowler states, man was to be "distinguished not by his rationality, nor by his moral sense, but by his religious character" (1980, p. 24).

The entrance of sin into human history did not remove man from his responsibility as God's servant, but man refused to acknowledge God's claim upon his life. He responded to God by serving the creature rather than the Creator; thus, man brought the wrath of God upon himself and the entire created order—producing division and strife, misery and death.

Through the death and resurrection of Jesus Christ, the entire creation-kingdom was redeemed and man, in the way of covenantal faith and obedience, was restored to his position, *coram deo*, i.e., before the face of God. Experiencing the power of Christ's redemption man again saw the meaning of life. He began to consecrate himself to his Creator and Redeemer, so that not only in his worship but also in the entirety of his life he was religiously directed lovingly to serve God according to His law and thus "to reclaim every sphere of life for the King" (Spykman, 1976, p.176).

Man was given an office by God to administer the creation in obedience to the law of the Creator. In fulfilling that office, man was to work not in isolation but in relationship with others as part of the human community. And, just as it structured other aspects of creation, so the law of God was to structure man's relationship with his fellow human beings.

Initially, the human community was undifferentiated; but, as mankind engaged in the work of developing and unfolding the creation, differentiation occurred:

> In the early chapters of Genesis, Adam is simply the general worker, equipped for every job, a man of all trades. In time, however, a degree of specialization becomes evident. Cain is a farmer, Abel a herdsman, Nimrod a hunter, Tubal a metal worker, and Tubal-Cain a musician. (McCarthy, et al, 1981, p. 159)

Throughout history different tasks and task-associations developed within society, according to the creational law of God—tasks and associations that were distinct according to their respective nature and function. In the Old Testament the tasks of the prophet, the priest, and the king come to more clearly differentiated expression. In the New Testament and by the end of the first century, the home, church, workplace, and state are seen as distinct entities. There is today, therefore, according to H. Henry Meeter:

> . . . a wide variety of distinct, though related spheres which arise out of the complex life of mankind, each having its own task to perform, its own mandate entrusted to it by God. Thus there exists the sphere of the family, the sphere of science, of art, of technique and invention, of trade and commerce, of industry, of agriculture, the sphere of the church, and, to mention no more, the sphere of things which belong to society as a whole. (1939, p. 159)

And within each of these spheres, we find a human community working religiously—obediently or disobediently—with a particular aspect of the created order.

Thus we discover in the Scriptures a pluralistic perspective that embraces the idea of social spheres within society. No sphere is subordinate to another. All spheres exist in a coordinate relationship to each other and are subordinate only to God. And, because they are all subordinate to God, the human communities within these spheres all function religiously before the face of God. This is why we say that life—not in part but the whole—is religion!

One of the spheres in society is the state, which is called upon to administer justice for all. The state does not act in a religiously neutral way. It functions according to a worldview that constantly shapes its social policy. This being the case, as the authors of *Society, State, and Schools* make clear, the state must face this decisive question:

> [W]hich world-view and which accompanying social paradigm offers the state the best promise of living up to its norm and central task, namely, to administer public justice evenhandedly with respect to all social structures and all confessional groups within society[?] (McCarthy et al, 1981, p. 166)

Another one of the spheres within society is the school, called upon to engage formally in "the process of gaining and transmitting insight" (Dordt College, 1979, p. 7). Religion is not incidental to this activity. In education, too,

> . . . man is fully man—not a mere data manipulator—and as such cannot but choose his ultimate point of reference and rest. This choice determines what he believes concerning himself and the nature of the world around him: it propels, guides and fashions also his theoretical activity. (ARSS, 1965, p. 8)

It's clear that academic life is religious.

Further, it should be noted that the state, because it is to administer justice with respect to all social structure, has a responsibility in regard to the school. It must not dominate the school. Instead, it must recognize that the school is a school and that it is the task of the state to protect the school from external intrusion, safeguarding the school's right to determine its religious direction and to make decisions of an academic nature. The "religious confessional plurality of school systems within society must be granted structural standing before the law" (McCarthy, et al, 1981, p. 167).

This is not to say that the state may no longer continue to operate the present public school system. But it should remove that system from its privileged status and recognize ". . . as a matter of just social policy the legal right of each faith community in society to work out its own world-view in a structured program of education" (McCarthy, et al, 1981, p. 168). In other words, the state and society in general should acknowledge that there is a place in our society for a school such as Dordt College—a school seeking in obedience to the Word of God to teach well what its students must know; a college that, although called "liberal arts," endeavors to provide insight that is serviceable in the kingdom; an institution that, although designated "Protestant evangelical," does seek from a Christian perspective to confront and speak to the issues of the day.

Yes, there is and must continue to be a place in our society for Dordt College.

## A Call

I realize, however, that just saying there is a place in our society for a school such as Dordt College does not guarantee the College's continuation in that place. Therefore, while I believe that the future of Dordt ultimately depends upon the blessing and favor of God, I would call upon those of you gathered here to join with me in the conviction that I have stated and described. I realize that presenting this call may seem a bit presumptuous; therefore, I want you to know that I hold all of you in high regard and present this call in all sincerity.

First, I call upon representatives of the American *public*—especially those in the political sector—to recognize and support the legitimacy of Dordt's place in society. This will not mean making provision for education that is inferior, for Dordt meets all the standards that have been set for acceptable educational achievement. Nor will this involve a violation of the principle of the separation of church and state. Dordt is not a church; it is a school, a college. Dordt is indeed a Christian college; but that does not mean that it is one of a number of private religious colleges existing alongside public colleges and universities that are non-religious. It means, according to the perspectival conviction we have articulated, that Dordt is one of a large group of academic institutions, all reflecting a religious worldview, all performing an important public service, and all deserving of impartial assistance. And, because Dordt holds membership in that academic community, I call upon you to recognize and support its legitimate place in our society.

Second, I call upon other *colleges* and *universities* to acknowledge Dordt's place. We join with you in a concern to render meaningful public service. We share with you a commitment to academic excellence. We certainly would not deny your right to function according to your particular worldview. We simply ask you to recognize our commitment to what we call "scripturally-oriented higher education" (Dordt College, 1967).

Third, I call upon the Dordt College *constituency* to join me in the conviction that there is a place for Dordt College in our society. I gratefully recognize that the establishment and development of the College—including the campus, student body, faculty, and staff—is ample testimony to your past and present commitment. But because of the problems and challenges mentioned earlier, that commitment is going to be sorely tested in the years that lie ahead. In 1937, you decided to work toward the establishment of a college that would function in harmony with Reformed principles. In doing so you said:

> The aim . . . is to give young people an education that is Christian, not merely in the sense that devotional exercises are appended to the ordinary work of the College, but in the larger and deeper sense that all the class work, all the students' intellectual, emotional, and imaginative activities shall be permeated with the spirit and teaching of Christianity. (Dordt College, 1979, p. 1)

I assume that you would say again today what you said in 1937. On the basis of that assumption, I call upon you to continue to support Dordt College as a visible expression of what you believe to be an obedient response to God's Word for education.

Fourth, I call upon the immediate *Dordt community*—board, administration, faculty, staff, and student body—to recognize that, if we would occupy the necessary and legitimate place described, we must be what we claim we are. In our statement of purpose we declare:

> As an institution of higher learning, Dordt College addresses itself to the task of Christian education. It seeks to acquire and transmit genuine

Christian insight, that is, to develop and implement an understanding of the entire creation in the liberating light of the Scriptures. Dordt College desires to be an institution of Christian learning for the benefit of both the attending student body and the entire Christian community, so that the Lord's Kingdom may come to greater expression. (Dordt College, 1979, p. 8)

This public declaration of purpose involves us in a commitment. Indeed, we are committed to balance the budget, keep the buildings in good repair, maintain high occupancy in the residence halls, preserve a satisfactory student-to-faculty ratio, and meet the demands of the accrediting agencies. But there is more, much more. The realization of our purpose and the maintenance of a distinct place for Dordt College will require that we, with Spirit-wrought energy, unitedly pursue our academic calling by taking heed to the Word of God, acknowledging His law to which every aspect of creation is subject, and bowing before the kingship of Christ in all our scientific work. Only if we are willing to do this may we expect society to recognize our place and our constituents to support us in our place.

**A Commitment**

I realize that this fourfold summons may appear a bit audacious. I dare to present it, however, because of a personal commitment that I now make public. I promise, in obedience to God, to work hard in the employment of whatever strength and talent God has given me, so that Dordt may be and increasingly become a college that serves the needs of society, reflects academic excellence, provides Christian education for covenant youth, and advances the cause of Christian scholarship. I promise, further, to perform my work not as a master but as a servant—aiding you in the fulfillment of your calling. As servant of God in your midst, I want to help constituents come to a clearer understanding of their duty in the sphere of education. I want to assist the Board in setting policies that reflect a biblical direction. I want to aid administrators in their supervisory activity. I want to support faculty members in gaining and transmitting insight, which will prepare students for kingdom service. I want to walk with students as they work to discover and develop their talents for the King.

I ask you to support me in this. I ask God to bless me in this, so that not only today but also tomorrow it may be recognized that in society—especially in the Christian community—there is indeed a place for Dordt College.

## References

Association for Reformed Scientific Studies (1965). *Scholarship in Biblical Perspective*. Hamilton, ON: Guardian Publishing.

Chambers, M. M. (August 25, 1980). "The Future of Higher Education," *The Chronicle of Higher Education*.

Crossland, F. E. (July/August, 1980). "Learning to Cope with a Downward Slope," *Change*.

Dordt College (1979). *The Educational Task of Dordt College*. By the Dordt College Faculty, Sioux Center, Iowa.

Dordt College (1967). *Scripturally-Oriented Higher Education*. By the Dordt College Faculty, Sioux Center, Iowa.

Fowler, S. (1980). *Issues in the Philosophy of Education*. Potchefstroom, S.A.: Potchefstroom University for Christian Higher Education.

Hesburgh, T. M. (April, 1981). "The Future of Liberal Education," *Change*.

Jencks, C. and Riesman, D. (1968). *The Academic Revolution*. New York: Doubleday.

McCarthy, R., et al. (1981). *Society, State, and Schools*. Grand Rapids, MI: Eerdmans.

Meeter, H. H. (1939). *Calvinism: An interpretation of its basic ideas*. Grand Rapids, MI: Zondervan.

Riesman, D. (1980). *On Higher Education: Origins and consequences of the counter-revolution in America*. San Francisco: Jossey-Bass.

Spykman, G. J. (1976). "Sphere-Sovereignty in Calvin and the Calvinist Tradition," in *Exploring the Heritage of John Calvin*, David Holwerda, ed. Grand Rapids, MI: Baker.

Stengel, R. (September 6, 1982). "Quality, not just Quantity," *Time*.

Winn, I. J. (June, 1980). "Turning the Screw: Higher education in the 1980s and 1990s," *Phi Beta Kappan*.

# Chapter Two

**To the Reader –**

In 1999, the International Association for the Promotion of Christian Higher Education (IAPCHE) planned a conference on "Christian World View and Scholarship" to be held at what was initially called Hilltop University in Mkar, Nigeria. I was serving as Executive Secretary of the Association and was assigned to present the keynote address on that topic at the conference. Even though we had had a successful conference at Daystar University in Nairobi, Kenya two years earlier, many predicted we would not be able to have a successful conference in Nigeria. Daystar was an established university whereas Hilltop was just getting started. Critics feared the university lacked the infrastructure to support a conference. But plans were completed and the conference was going to be held in January.

To make good use of time and money, an extensive trip was arranged for me to travel on behalf of the Association to St. Petersburg, Russia, and Amsterdam before the conference in Mkar, Nigeria and to San Jose, Costa Rica after the conference. The whole trip, including the conference, was going to take at least three weeks. Since it was mid-winter in Northwest Iowa, I drove to Sioux Falls the evening before my scheduled departure and stayed in a motel to make sure that I would be available early the next worming. As it turned out, when I arrived at the airport, I was told that my flight had been cancelled because of an incoming snow storm and that my departure would be delayed for at least one day. I decided that rather than stay in Sioux Falls another day, I would go home. On my way the blizzard hit, and driving was difficult. I was on the last part of my journey home when I was caught in a "white-out," drove into a huge snowdrift, and ended up unconscious in a ditch. A trucker stopped and, rather than calling an ambulance and wrecker, he helped me to his truck and drove me home. When she saw me, Louise realized I had to go to the emergency room at the hospital. The examining doctor said I had a severe concussion, and it would be impossible for me to take the trip I had planned. When I argued with him, telling him about the important speech I was scheduled to give in Mkar, Nigeria, he wasn't impressed and told Louise to take me directly home and put me to bed.

Our daughter, Susan DeYoung, was working with me for the Association; she saw to the cancellation of the various flights. She also arranged to have Dr.

John Kok, a Dordt College philosophy professor—who was also scheduled to speak at the conference—read my keynote address. Published reports indicate that the conference was a surprising success and that the keynote was well-received—due in large part, I am sure, to the speaking ability of Dr. Kok. To this day, I am grateful for his willingness to step into a difficult situation.

# CHRISTIAN WORLD VIEW AND SCHOLARSHIP

Even though this is my first visit to Hilltop, it is not my first visit to Nigeria. In 1981 I was invited to this country to address two conferences—first, a meeting of Christian school administrators and teachers and, second, an annual gathering of Christian Reformed Church missionaries and their families in Jos, just prior to the beginning of the Hillcrest school year. Although it was an exhausting three weeks, it is an experience I have treasured.

One event that stands out in my memory occurred on the first evening of my visit. I was in a Mission Guest House, talking with a Nigerian pastor whom I had just met. During the course of our conversation, I asked him: "What is the greatest and most immediate need of the Christian community in Nigeria today?" I expected him to mention the need for more church buildings, pastors, evangelists, and translations of Scripture. To my surprise, however, and without hesitation, he responded: "Our greatest need is for an institution of Christian higher education where we and our youth may be trained to understand the implications of the Christian faith not only for the church, but for other areas of life as well." Being directly involved in the work of Christian higher education, I was thrilled with this response and shared it with many of my associates upon returning to the United States.

Since that time, with the blessing of the Lord and the help of the Christian community-at-large—including the Friends of Hilltop in North America—you have been able to establish your institution of Christian higher education. We rejoice with you in this and pray that through this school and its academic program the Lord will bring you, as the Nigerian pastor said, to understand the implications of the Christian faith for all of life and learning.

Today, just a few years after its beginning, we meet for this regional conference at Hilltop. All of you should know that two years ago in this very month, a similar conference concerning "Christian World View and Scholarship" was held at Daystar University in Nairobi, Kenya. One of

---

IAPCHE Hilltop Conference, Mkar, Nigeria, January, 1999.

the leaders of that conference was Professor Godfrey Nguru, Daystar's vice chancellor for academic affairs, who is also with us and will speak to this conference. The meetings in Nairobi were highly successful, especially in developing a sense of community among the approximately 100 persons present. Therefore, at the conclusion of the Daystar Conference, it was decided that another conference, with a similar theme, should be held elsewhere in Africa. Knowing that Hilltop had just been established, and assuming that you would want to be part of this communal effort to promote the perspective involved in "Christian World View and Scholarship," it was decided that this was the ideal place and time for the next conference to be held.

We thank God that we can be here together. We have met in the assurance and conviction that there are many who support our efforts and who are praying for the Lord's blessing on us as we seek to gain further insight into the meaning and implications of a Christian worldview for our academic work.

**Theme**

The theme of this keynote address is the same as that of the conference: "Christian World View and Scholarship." I will have more to say about the theme later; but now I wish to observe that this is an excellent and important theme. It is important for Hilltop and other institutions of Christian higher education, important for Christian scholars in Christian and non-Christian institutions. It is important for the International Association for the Promotion of Christian Education (IAPCHE), which recognizes in the statement of its Basis that scholarship does not and cannot have a neutral, uncommitted character, but should be pursued from a biblical perspective.

In a paper titled "Church in Society," John C. Vanderstelt (Dordt College) demonstrates the importance of worldview for the instituted church. He does so by observing that we can become so engrossed in internal programs and problems that we are unable to see the place and the task of the church in human society. Then, when confronted with attacks on the Christian faith, the church is tempted to resort to all kinds of unscriptural attitudes and positions. Therefore, says Vanderstelt, the church must "learn anew to discern the Father's will." In other words, the church must learn a new direction, perspective, worldview that will enable her to articulate "in contemporary fashion . . . a biblical way of living in which humans work, think, decide, eat, and believe as obedient children of their heavenly Father" (Vanderstelt, 1996, pp. 26–27).

The same must be said for Christian scholars and institutions of Christian higher education. We can become so involved with immediate, practical matters—also in initiating and maintaining our institutions—that we lose sight of the true nature of our academic calling. Then, especially when under attack, we can easily respond in terms of "unscriptural philosophies so prominent in secularized scholarship" (Vanderstelt, 1996, p. 27). Therefore, it is essential that we continually seek to reform, reshape, and reformulate our ways of thinking and teaching according to a Christian, biblical worldview.

Having noted the importance of our subject, I would like to comment briefly on the theme "Christian World View and Scholarship" and, in the process, set forth the outline for this address. It appears that the theme contains at least three sub-themes that call for our attention:

1. Worldview
   What does it mean?
   To what extent are any or all of us directed by a worldview?
   How do our worldviews differ?
2. Christian Worldview
   There are many Christian worldviews.
   By which Christian worldview should we be governed?
3. Scholarship
   How should scholarship be understood?
   Should we speak or think in terms of Christian worldview and scholarship?
   In what way should a Christian worldview reflect itself in our scholarship?

Since entire books have been written on Christian worldview and scholarship, it is obviously not my intent to attempt an exhaustive treatment of this subject. Following the direction of the brief outline given above, I will seek to make some meaningful observations concerning this subject and, in the process, provide a context in which others can also make their presentations in light of the conference theme.

## Worldview

What is it? What does it mean? What do we have in mind when we speak of worldview?

Some time ago, John Suk, editor of *The Banner* (official publication of the Christian Reformed Church of North America) wrote a series of articles about "What it Means to be Reformed." In his November 18,

1996 editorial, titled "Tending Your Worldview" he used the windshield of a car as an illustration:

> ... take time to clean your windshield, at least if you want to see where you are going. The drive ... will be safe and pleasurable only in proportion to how well you can see.
>
> The Christian life is like that. If you want to follow Jesus, you must keep your eyes on Him as well as see the world for what it really is. To do that you must have the right worldview.
>
> Everyone has a world view. It is the intellectual equipment you need in order to live. (Suk, 1996, p. 4)

For our purposes, we might add that a worldview is also the intellectual equipment needed for scholarship, i.e., to study, teach, and learn. In the *Institutes of the Christian Religion,* John Calvin observes:

> ... as persons who are old, or whose eyes are by any means become dim, if you show them the most beautiful book, though they perceive something written, but can scarcely read two words together, yet, by the assistance of spectacles, will begin to read distinctively,—so the Scripture, collecting in our minds the otherwise confused notions of Deity, dispels the darkness, and gives us a clear view of the true God. (1936, I, vi, 1, p. 80)

Abraham Kuyper, speaking of the teachings of Calvin and his articulation of biblical principles, describes Calvinism as a "life system" that gives us insight into the three fundamental relations of all human life: our relation to God, to mankind, and to the world (1943, p. 19). It is clear that Kuyper's "life system" was intended as an equivalent to the German *weltanschauung,* usually translated "worldview" in English (Heslam, 1998, p. 88).

In line with Calvin and Kuyper, Albert M. Wolters (Redeemer University College) describes the development of a biblical, reformational worldview as the desire to live by Scripture alone. Wolters sees worldview as rooted in and determined by faith and defines it as "the comprehensive framework of one's basic beliefs about things" (1985, p. 2). Wolters goes on to analyze his definition by noting that "things" refers to everything about which it is possible to have a belief; "beliefs" are not hypotheses but convictions that one is willing to defend or promote with the endurance of hardship; "basic beliefs" have to do with ultimate questions, matters of principle and a "framework" that acknowledges that the various aspects of a worldview hang together with a tendency toward pattern and coherence.

I find Wolters' definition and analyses very helpful, especially when he goes on to describe the role that worldview plays in our lives:

> ... our worldview functions as a guide to our life. A worldview, even when it is half unconscious and unarticulated, functions like a compass or a road map. It orients us in the world at large, gives us a sense of what is up and what is down, what is right and what is wrong in the confusion of events and phenomena that confronts us. Our worldview shapes, to a significant degree, the way we assess the events, issues and structures of our civilization and our times. It allows us to "place" or "situate" the various phenomena that come into our purview. (1985, p. 4)

Working out of a perspective similar to that of Wolters, James Olthuis of the Institute for Christian Studies in Toronto, describes a worldview as a vision for life, "a framework or set of fundamental beliefs through which we view the world and our calling and future in it" (1989, p. 29). He goes on to state that worldviews arise out of faith, which gives rise to a vision of the whole of reality. Then, having noted that worldview functions both descriptively and normatively, Olthuis summarizes with these words:

> ... it is this rootedness of worldviews in faith that gives them their this-is-the-way-it-is-and-should-be character. As a vision "of" faith "for" life and the world, a worldview first shapes itself to faith and then shapes the world to itself, projecting images of the cosmic order on the plane of human experience. The basic tenets of a worldview are not argued to but argued from. (1989, p. 32)

Having come to some understanding of what we mean by worldview, we must go on to ask, "Who has a worldview?" In his editorial, John Suk takes the position that "everyone has a world view" (1996, p. 4). Is that true? Does everyone have a worldview?

Wolters (1985, p. 4) is quite emphatic in making the point that everyone does have a worldview: "In general, therefore, everyone has a worldview, however inarticulate he or she may be in expressing it. Having a worldview is simply part of being an adult human being." Brian J. Walsh (University of Toronto) and J. Richard Middleton (University of Guelph) hold to the same position. As does Wolters, Walsh and Middleton insist that to be human is to have a worldview:

> Humans are creatures of vision. This does not mean simply that they have eyes. Animals have eyes. Rather, it means that we are creatures who live our lives in terms of our perspective, our vision of life. Animals need no such perspective, for they are guided by instincts. Humans make life choices, and they make them in terms of their way of looking at things. (1984, p. 31)

In other words, humans—all human beings—make life choices in terms of their worldview.

This point must be emphasized. The question is not, "Do we or should we have a worldview?" Everyone has a worldview, a perspective, a vision of life. To be human is to have a worldview. The question is, "What is the nature of our worldview?" Again, everyone has a worldview; but these worldviews differ.

I was reminded of this while reading *Genesis* by Bill Moyers. Moyers (1996) reports on conversations with people from various confessional backgrounds concerning the stories in the first book of the Bible, the book of Genesis. These people—some of them well known in the world of Christian higher education, e.g., Roberta Hestenes and Lewis Smedes—reflected many and different worldviews. It was clear that these different worldviews produced or resulted in many different understandings and interpretations of the Bible, as well as in many different perspectives on life.

Living and working in a postmodern age as we do, we might be inclined to give equal standing to all of these different perspectives or worldviews. It is my contention, however, that we should not move in this direction. It may be true that postmodernism has shown that the claims of rationalistic or secular humanism on behalf of autonomous human reason are false. As David Hoekema (1996, p. 9) of Calvin College has indicated: "Postmodernism has pulled back the curtain in the wizard's chamber, and the human role in all scholarship stands exposed for all to see." Still, we find it difficult to agree with Dale D. Soden and Kathleen H. Storm (1996) of Whitworth College, who suggest ". . . the Christian might welcome the advent of postmodernism into the late twentieth century intellectual methods." To the contrary, we should be warned concerning postmodernism, primarily because of its relativism. While it has made clear that everyone works out of a certain perspective, postmodernism, in the name of pluralism and/or multiculturalism, is skeptical about the possibility of absolute truth and tends to regard every perspective as equally worthy of consideration. David F. Wells, of Gordon-Conwell Seminary comments on this in *No Place for Truth:*

> The loss of an overarching purpose . . . has deeply affected most academic fields . . . . The Old Enlightenment orthodoxy that a rational, objective scholarship is possible has itself fallen prey to what the Enlightenment unleashed. In the absence of assent to a body of universal truth, objectively discovered truths often reflect only the interests and dispositions of the scholars concerned. In a climate of relativism, it becomes quite dif-

ficult to insist on the universal viability of one's findings, even in science ... the days when your conclusion could be accorded normativity for anyone else are gone. (1993, p. 65)

Vigorous though it may be, the judgment of James Leffel of Ohio Dominican College, regarding postmodernism seems to ring true:

> Truth, declares a growing collective consciousness, is relative: what is true, right, or beautiful for one person is not necessarily true, right, or beautiful for another. Relativism (postmodernism) says that truth is not fixed by outside reality, but is decided by a group of individuals for themselves. Truth is not discovered, but manufactured. Truth is ever changing not only in insignificant matters of taste or fashion, but also in crucial matters of spirituality, morality and reality itself. (1996, p. 31)

In *Contours of a World View*, Arthur F. Holmes (Wheaton College) takes a much different approach than the postmodernist. Commenting on the various worldviews, he observes that "Christian theism and naturalistic or secular humanism are the primary options of the day." Holmes goes on to note that these options stand in antithetical relationship to one another. Secular humanism

> ... views persons as a part and product of the physical world, and it limits values to what has value for humankind. ... It denies any theistic basis for human worth, for values in general, and for hope and meaning in this life. The secular humanist's source of hope is entirely immanent in nature and humanity and cannot transcend their limitations, rather than being located outside of nature and man in a transcendent God. (1983, pp. 17–18)

Holmes then observes that the secular humanist worldview also produces scientism, i.e., "the view that *scientific knowledge* can be applied to the solution of all our problems, as well as to the testing of all human beliefs and moral judgments" (1983, p. 18).

In bold contrast to secular humanism stands the worldview of Christian theism. In this connection, Holmes (1983, p. 13) quotes James Orr who, in *The Christian View of God and the World*, addresses the overall character of a Christian view of things. The main design, he announced, is to show

> that there is a definite Christian view of things, which has a character, coherence, and unity of its own, and stands in sharp contrast with counter theories and speculations, and that this world-view ... can amply justify itself at the bar of both history and of experience.

In *Issues in the Philosophy of Education*, Stuart Fowler notes Holmes' observation that Christian theism and secular humanism stand in antithetical relationship to one another. In a section titled "The Way of Religious Antithesis," he writes that in turning to Scripture we learn that "the key to the whole cosmos is religion" (1980, p. 24). Created in the image of God, the human heart is continually, inescapably confronted with the revelation, i.e., the Word of God. Among other things, this means that religious commitment—either for or against God and His Word—is prior to every human activity. Therefore, any activity, any thought that is not subject to God's Word is necessarily subject to an idol, the deification of an aspect of the creation.

Walsh and Middleton describe this Christian view of things (Orr), this perspective that is subject to God's Word (Fowler), as the biblical worldview of creation, fall, and redemption. It is a comprehensive view that "tells with clarity and richness who we are, where we are, what is wrong and what the remedy is. It is a vision that illuminates literally all of life and empowers us to walk obediently before the Lord" (Walsh et al., p. 93).

I believe enough has been said to make clear that, in speaking of "Christian World View and Scholarship," we must think primarily in terms of the options described by Fowler, i.e., subjection to the Word of God or subjection to an idol. Moreover, since it is our purpose, in the words of Wolters, "to live by Scripture alone" (1985, p. 1), we move on to consider what is involved in a biblical, Christian worldview.

**Christian worldview**

At this point, we must acknowledge that, as there are many worldviews (in general), so there are many Christian worldviews (in particular). This is evident, for example, in *Christ and Culture,* in which H. Richard Niebuhr (1956) develops five alternative views of culture, i.e., five alternative worldviews:

1. Christ *against* culture. This is the perspective of *opposition*, in which the Christian faith is called to distance itself from culture. One cannot be a friend of God and the culture of the times.
2. Christ *of* culture. This is the perspective of *accommodation*, in which the Christian faith is expected to adjust to culture. Christianity and contemporary culture are potentially, at least, in agreement with each other.
3. Christ *above* culture. This is the perspective of *dualism*, in which faith belongs to a higher, supernatural order and culture belongs to a lower, natural order. The Christian faith adds to

and completes what culture cannot accomplish.
4. Christ *and* culture. This is the perspective of *paradox*, in which there is a tension between the Christian faith and culture. In this view, Christianity belongs to the kingdom of God and culture belongs to the kingdom of this world.
5. Christ, the *transformer* of culture. This is the perspective of *transformation* or *reformation*, in which the Christian faith is seen as changing culture for the better. In this view, Christianity seeks to implement in culture the redeeming, reformational work of God in Jesus Christ.

The implications of these alternative worldviews for Christianity and scholarship are quite evident:

1. Christ *against* culture implies that Christians must *isolate* themselves from the sciences.
2. Christ *of* culture suggests that the best of current scholarship can easily be *merged* with the Christian faith.
3. Christ *above* culture would seem to claim that scientific insight is accessible to unaided human reason, but that the Christian faith—more specifically Christian dogma or doctrine—functions as the *criterion* of ultimate truth for all branches of scholarship.
4. Christ *and* culture describes Christian faith and scholarship as occupying two realms that stand in *paradoxical* relationship to one another. Scholarship, belonging to the worldly realm, actually lies under divine judgment.
5. Christ *transforming* culture views the Christian faith as seeking the *transformation* or *reformation* of culture, including the work and products of scholarship.

It is obvious, then, that the first four positions or worldviews—Christ *against, of, above, and* culture—because of their basic dualism do not encourage Christians to be involved in changing society or scholarship for the better. Gordon Spykman, of Calvin College, emphasizes this point in his "Critique":

> In retrospect, the following critical comments are applicable to the first four positions reviewed above. All four involve a dual normativity, which betrays or at least compromises the biblical exhortation against every sort of divided allegiance. They lend a certain legitimacy, furthermore, to viewing some sectors of life, including scholarship, as sinful or natural, or unredeemed. Accordingly, in these views there is a severely limited

> acknowledgment of the effects of evil in the world, as well as of the renewing grace of God and the lordship of Jesus Christ. They therefore also impose unwarranted restrictions upon the field of Christian scholarship. (1985, p. 5)

At the same time, the alternative view—moving out from the fifth position, i.e., the *transformational* or *reformational*—aims at overcoming these dualistic problems by proposing a more unified perspective on Christian scholarship.

Having presented his "Critique," Spykman goes on in a subsequent chapter to describe four contemporary views—reflecting the influence of the Enlightenment of the eighteenth century—in dealing with the relationship between biblical revelation and Christian scholarship that are also helpful in understanding the issue before us (1985, pp. 7–9). The four views are:

1. *Compartmentalists* who operate in two universes of discourse, acknowledging one norm for their faith life and another for their scholarship. For example, as Christian persons such scholars may hold confessionally to some form of creationism, while at the same time propounding a form of evolutionism in their scientific methodologies.
2. *Concordists*, who operate in two universes of discourse, insisting that the two can be harmonized, e.g., the Bible and science supplement or even complement each other like the two halves that make up a whole.
3. *Externalists* who also operate in two universes of discourse but claim that common grace creates a measure of common ground among members of the scientific community. Ultimately, the Christian faith and science enjoy only an external relationship. Faith does not affect the internal operations or functions of the scientific process.
4. *Integralists* who reject the two universes of discourse, calling for the "inner reformation" of the sciences—not only of theology, but also of all the sciences. The entire scientific enterprise must be directed by biblical revelation. The claims of Scripture rest upon every academic endeavor in a radical, integral, and comprehensive way.

In light of the above, it should be evident that, as we must work out of a transformational perspective on the relationship between Christ and culture, we must function in terms of an *integralist* view of the relationship between biblical revelation and Christian scholarship. It should also be clear that, if we would develop a Christian worldview on scholarship, we must begin with the Bible, the inscripturated Word of God.

In 1965, at the King's College, Briarcliff Manor, New York, USA, Paul G. Schrotenboer delivered a lecture at a meeting of the American Scientific Affiliation under the title, "Integral Christian Scholarship." In the course of his lecture, Schrotenboer stated:

> You will understand that an association which claims scripturally directed learning for its purpose could hardly, in explaining itself, first relate itself to the field of learning and later on bring Scripture in as an afterthought. This would belie the avowed purpose as a structural principle. For this reason, we have started with the message of Scripture. (1965, p. 3)

This, of course, is what we want to do: we want to avoid bringing the Bible in as an afterthought. Therefore, we begin with the Bible, and we are also encouraged to do so by literature that is more recent. For example, Mark A. Noll, of Wheaton College, concludes his book, *The Scandal of the Evangelical Mind*, by stating:

> ... attachment to Scripture is the place to begin.... To pursue the Bible, as it reveals God-in-human flesh, is to find not just Christ but the world that Christ created, the humanity that He joined, and the beauty that He embodied in Himself. (1994, pp. 250-251)

Therefore, Walsh and Middleton observe:

> For Christians, the ultimate criterion by which we judge our world view is the Bible. It is God's revelation of reality. Paul tells Timothy that the Scriptures have a purpose; they are to teach, reprove and correct us, and to train us in righteousness so that we may be equipped for a life of good work (2 Timothy 3:16–17). If we seek a world view that leads to life and not death, then we must go to the Scriptures for instruction. And as our world view is informed, corrected and shaped by the Scriptures under the guidance of the Spirit, we receive direction for our way of life. (1984, p. 39)

Again—indeed, guided by the Holy Spirit—we must turn to Scripture as our starting point. Given the reality of sin and its effects—also upon our understanding—we must, as we observed earlier, with John Calvin, put on the spectacles of Scripture to make sure we are seeing correctly.

Beginning with the Bible, we learn—from the Bible—that, while there is but one Word of God, that word comes to us or manifests itself to us in three ways, forms, or modes:

1. *Creationally.* God's creation is revelatory: "The heavens declare the glory of God; the skies proclaim the work of his hands" (Psalm 19:1). From the creation, we understand how God's Word holds for creation, for all His varied creatures, and for the various life-relationships of humankind as image bearers of God in His world.
2. *Inscripturated.* To counteract the consequences of our fall into sin, God republished His Word redemptively in the Bible. This, the written Word, has been given to reveal Christ to us and to redirect our misdirected lives, reforming that which has been deformed by sin—including the reformation of our deformed academic enterprises.
3. *Personified* in Jesus Christ. The Word that was in the beginning, that was God, ". . . became flesh and lived for a while among us" (John 1:14). He is the Mediator of creation and redemption. He is the key to the meaning of the world, the creation.

It should not be supposed that these distinctions are insignificant. In many traditions, there has been a tendency to reduce the fullness of God's Word to one of its manifestations. For example, classic *liberals* limit the idea of revelation to the rabbi, Jesus of Nazareth. As the Master teacher, He exemplifies the universal fatherhood of God and brotherhood of man. Therefore, we should follow in His steps. In a different way, *neo-orthodoxy* also reduces the Word of God to the Word incarnate in Jesus Christ. Since, according to Karl Barth, revelation is exclusively a "personal act" of God, the creation and the Bible are not revelatory in a direct sense. They only serve as "pointers" and "witnesses" to the Word of God incarnate.

*Evangelical* Christians tend to limit God's Word to the Bible, with Jesus Christ viewed only as personal Savior and Lord and the creation only as the arena for the struggle between sin and grace. *Naturalists*—if even aware of revelation—restrict revelation to "mother nature." Nevertheless, in each case—liberalism, neo-orthodoxy, evangelicalism, and naturalism—the Word of God is reduced to Christ, the Bible, or creation, and is, therefore, limited as the Christo-centric basis for Christian scholarship.

Only when we recognize Christ, the incarnate Word, as the key to God's Word for creation and as the heart of His Word inscripturated will we be able to begin to "take captive every thought to make it obedient to Christ" (2 Corinthians 10:5). By the impinging power of His *creational*

Word, God in His preserving grace still maintains the structural order of the cosmos—which makes science possible. By the light of the *inscripturated* Word, He redirects our hearts to renewed academic obedience. In the Word *incarnate*, who now claims "all authority in heaven and on earth" (Matthew 28:18), He reminds us in whose service we stand.

From the Bible we learn "the basic realities of our cultural and societal experience," (Wolters, 1985, p. 11), i.e., the biblical themes of creation, fall, and redemption:

1. *Creation.* In the beginning, by His Word, God created the heavens and the earth, and He declared the creation "good," i.e., it fulfilled the purpose for which it was made. In creating, God brought into being His kingdom, which He ruled by His Word. He also made man/woman in His image, capable of responding to His Word as citizens of His kingdom. Thus, He covenanted with man/woman to be His servants—dressing and keeping, ruling and caring for creation as His representatives—promising life if they obeyed and death if they disobeyed His kingdom Word.

2. *Fall.* Instead of obeying, man/woman disobeyed, broke covenant with God, declaring their independence from Him. Instead of worshipping and serving the Creator, they worshipped and served the creature or some aspect of the creation. Thus, they became guilty of idolatry (Romans 1:23, 25). Bringing the curse of the fall upon themselves, as well as upon the rest of creation, man/woman continued to be servants, but they were "bound to a despot who rules over a kingdom of slaves" (Walsh, et al., 1984, p. 70).

3. *Redemption.* In faithfulness to His covenant, God immediately responded to Satan's illegitimate claims by announcing the first clue concerning His redemptive plan: "And I will put enmity between you and the woman, and between your offspring and hers; he will crush your head, and you will strike his heel" (Genesis 3:15). This announcement, this promise, was fulfilled in the fullness of time through the birth, suffering, death, resurrection, and ascension of Jesus Christ—by means of which He restored the entire creation as the kingdom and the redeemed as the citizens of the kingdom of God.

The following words of Wolters help us to summarize what we have just stated:

> In a few bold strokes, we have sketched the outline of a biblical worldview, stressing the breadth and range of creation and the effects of sin and salvation on that creation in its fullest extent. We have seen that these central realities—creation, fall and redemption—are the fundamental points of the biblical compass. When we look through the corrective lens of Scripture, everywhere the things of our experience begin to reveal themselves as *creaturely*, as under the curse of *sin*, and as longing for *redemption*. These are the ABC's of authentically Christian experience, the biblical assumptions that clarify our experience when we bring every thought into obedience in Jesus Christ. (1985, p. 72)

Wolters could have added that these are the biblical assumptions that clarify our experience when we bring every thought into obedience to Jesus Christ, also and *especially in the world of scholarship*.

Having started with the Bible, and having come to some understanding of what is involved in a biblical worldview, we move now to a consideration of:

## Scholarship

Before dealing with the substance of this third and last section, I want to make two clarifying observations:

1. When speaking of "scholarship," I have in mind scholarship not in the narrow but in the broad sense of "education," i.e., scholarship that includes research and teaching or instruction. I believe it is appropriate to do so. As Harold Heie, of Gordon College, observes in *Conversations for Christian Higher Education*, it is the proper calling of the academic at a Christian college "to be a *teacher* and a *scholar*" (1996, p. 33). Considering the context of this conference and looking at the rest of the program, I gather also that you expected me to consider scholarship in the broad rather than in the narrow sense.

2. I want to emphasize that in speaking of Christian worldview and scholarship, we are in this address concerned primarily with the significance of a Christian worldview for *scholarship* and *education*, and not for Christian life in general—important though the Christian life may be and is. One of the dangers of moralistic dualism is that it promotes the idea that Christian education is simply a matter of a Christian professor teaching a class of Christian students. Of course, this is not the case. It is essential that the professors are Christian, and there also may be something very attractive about having all the students be

committed Christians. But what about the subjects that are being taught? They, too, must be "touched" by the Word of God. Otherwise, we run the risk of having "schizophrenic" education, i.e., a school, college, or university with Christian professors, Bible studies, and chapel services, but courses and a curriculum that remain closed to the reforming power of the Word of God.

Having made these two observations and moving on to consider the implications of a Christian worldview for educational and academic activity, we must inquire concerning the *purpose* of this educational activity. In light of what we have observed earlier concerning the biblical vision of the kingdom of God, I would suggest that it is the purpose of our educational, academic activity to seek to understand and transmit an understanding of the creation and its history. This is so that kingdom citizens may understand the creation and their place in it, and their calling to bring to expression the kingdom rule of Jesus Christ over all things. This is what Spykman seems to have in mind when he wrote:

> ... the following can serve as a compressed definition of Christian scholarship in its various branches: a) seeking to discern the norms of God's Word for creation as they hold for our life together in his world; b) illumined and redirected by God's Word in the Scriptures; c) under the rule of God's Word in our Lord Jesus Christ; and d) in the service of his coming kingdom. (1985, p. 19)

In this connection, I would suggest that, instead of speaking about Christian worldview *and* scholarship, we should speak of Christian worldview *on* or *for* scholarship. B. J. van der Walt, of Potchefstroom University for Christian Higher Education, is correct when he writes: "Man does not as a Christian practice scholarship and *in addition* to it also serve God . . . "(1997, p. 31). As Walsh and Middleton point out:

> ... scholarship is religious . . . . Since scholarship is ultimately rooted in religious commitment . . . the question is not really one of "integrating" faith and scholarship. Faith and scholarship always *are* integrated. The only real question is, *Which faith?* Many Christians, unaware of the implicitly religious nature of scholarship, find themselves doing scholarship from a faith perspective which is antithetical to their Christian faith. To do scholarship Christianly, then, is to consciously allow our faith to direct our studies. (1984, p. 172)

What does it mean to allow our faith, in this case our Christian worldview, "to direct our studies," our academic work? What does this involve?

Ultimately a biblical, reformational worldview calls for a biblical, reformational *philosophy* that can relate the basic insights of a biblical perspective to the special disciplines of the academic enterprise. I have in mind, for example, the reformational philosophies of scholars such as D. H. T. Vollenhoven and Herman Dooyeweerd of The Netherlands. It is not our purpose here to describe or articulate such a philosophy. We can, however, in a preliminary way present the implications of a biblical worldview for our scholarly academic work.

First, it should be clear from what we have said to this point that we, as Christians, are called to the *sanctification* of our academic work. It is not enough simply to dedicate our work to the service of God, to demonstrate some essential connection between our work and the Christian faith, or to add a bit of Christianity to "neutral" academic activity. Instead, qualified by the Holy Spirit and directed by the Word, we must see to the internal renewal, the inner reformation of the sciences. This will involve us, of course, in the *ongoing* and *progressive* renewal of our academic work. Rather than thinking only in terms of scholarship, we must engage in the ongoing reformation of the sciences, i.e., we must take that which was *formed* at creation and *deformed* by sin, and continually work at seeing to it that it is *reformed* in Christ—reformed from within.

Second, as we engage in this ongoing, reformational academic activity, our point of departure must be the *creation order* and the recognition that "the Creator's sustaining and governing hand is not absent from the many ways in which human beings organize their living together" (Wolters 1985, p. 80). It is clear from Scripture that God has formed or established a structural order for the family, church, and state. It is also clear from viewing society in light of Scripture that He has established an order for such institutions as the school and business. Each institution has its own distinct nature and creational structure; each institution is a positivization (putting into practice a creational norm) of the creational structure that holds for it. The nature and structure of an institution also defines its authority. Each institution has authority within its own sphere; but that authority is from God, who alone is sovereign and in authority over all. The all-pervasive *deforming* effects of sin are seen when there is a perversion of the norms for a particular sphere, e.g., injustice in the state; or when the authority of one sphere is extended to and over another sphere, e.g., the state limits or denies the freedom of the academy.

Third, taking advantage of insights articulated by reformational thought, it must be said that the *academy* is the place for theoretical reflection upon creational reality. That is its unique window upon God's world, God's creation. Such reflection or analysis defines the academy's peculiar *reforming* tasks. The entire creation is within the academy's scholarly purview. Nothing—whether organic or inorganic, whether belonging to the plant, animal, or human kingdom—is to be excluded. Russell Maatman, of Dordt College, has observed that God "created everything that chemists study" (1998). It should also be noted, however, that everything that God created falls within the academy's sphere of responsibility *and* that this responsibility is to be fulfilled in an academic manner. As Spykman has stated:

> ... to each its own. For the academy this means focusing on systematic inquiry, experimentation, evaluation and directives for reformation. The academy may, for instance, study banking, but it is not a bank. It may study family life, but it is not a family. It may study the political process, but it is not a political organization. Primarily and centrally, the academy is for theoretical inquiry aiming at getting things straight (reformation). (1985, p. 71)

Among other things, Spykman could have added to his list that the Christian academy may study the doctrines of the church, but it is not a church—it is an academy, engaged in theoretical, academic activity.

Fourth, it should be noted that the creation order is brought into the academy through or by means of the *curriculum*. Therefore, the content of the curriculum is not to be decided in an arbitrary or pragmatic fashion; rather, it is to be anchored in a principled and structured view of created reality.

> A biblical perspective on Christian scholarship accordingly points in the direction of the creational order. The various disciplines are then definable as theoretical inquiries into the various aspects of created reality. Thus each discipline (within the curriculum) focusses on its peculiar facet of our life together in God's world with its numerous creatures great and small, its inorganic materials, plant life, animals, human culture and conduct, and our various societal institutions. Biologists, for example, deal with the biotic aspect of created reality, the psychologists with the psychic aspect, the linguist with the lingual aspect, the ethicist with the moral aspect, and so on. (Spykman. 1985, p. 72)

As such, the curriculum should also reflect, as John Van Dyk (1978, pp. 4-8), of Dordt College, has indicated, a three-dimensional *coherence*:

1. The coherence between the Creator and His creation. While God must be distinguished from creation, He must not be separated from creation. Thus, what we are considering in the natural sciences, social sciences, and humanities is a created

order that was not only brought into existence by the power of God's Word, but is also upheld moment by moment by the powerful Word of God.
2. The coherence within the creation. There is unity as well as diversity within the created order. The diversity of creation is reflected by the various subjects within the curriculum; but the unity of creation is demonstrated when the curriculum reflects the interrelatedness, the connections between the various disciplines and subjects.
3. The coherence between theory and practice. The Greeks placed a wide gap between theory and practice, knowing and doing. It is a fact that, according to a Christian worldview, the purpose of education is to enable kingdom citizens to understand the creation and their place and calling in it. It therefore seems clear that we must recapture the biblical notion that knowing and doing are closely related. Consider, for example, Psalm 111:10: "The fear of the Lord is the beginning of wisdom; all who follow His precepts have good understanding." The following are some examples of what we mean:

> . . . when we teach science we must teach the ability to exercise Christian stewardship over all God's good creation. When we teach social studies we must teach not only what is the case in our society, but also what *ought* to be the case in our society. In other words, our graduates should be the kind of people who will be able to offer Christian insight and healing in our economic, political, and social worlds. And when we teach history, we not only teach the facts of history, we also teach our students how to cope with and how to counteract the spirits that have through historical processes taken hold of our civilization. (Van Dyk, 1978, p. 8)

In other words, when the curriculum provides the interrelatedness of both theoretical and practical insight, students are enabled to understand theoretically and implement practically the great commandment that we, through loving God and neighbor, must seek first the kingdom of God.

Finally, we must note that anchoring the curriculum in the creation order creates a context for *communal scholarship*. Recognizing the intricate interrelatedness of the creation and, therefore, the various sciences, Christian scholars and educators must work together as members of a team. In this way, they will be able to share insights and support one another in their work and, in the process, open up the connections among the various subjects and disciplines. Working out of the creation order also creates a common arena for *dialogue* among scholars of differing schools of thought—believers and unbelievers alike. It is what Nicholas Wolterstorff of Yale University, calls "cross-perspectival conversation" (1993, pp. 119, 124). The creation order lays claim on all educators; its structures are common to all. As we have seen, the spiritual antithesis of which the Bible speaks is very real in the academic arena. At the same time, however, there are common structures of creation that hold for all in every branch of learning.

What does this mean for those working out of a Christian worldview in the academy? It means at least:

1. That we can and must participate in the broad, contemporary academic conversation;
2. That we can and must participate in the academic conversation, wholeheartedly committed to a Christian worldview that recognizes the lordship of Jesus Christ (Incarnate Word) and takes seriously the creational order (Creational Word), all in the light of biblical revelation (Inscripturated Word);
3. That we, along with the rest of the Christian community, can work in obedience to the *cultural mandate* of Genesis 1 and the *great commission* of Matthew 28, recognizing Christ's unlimited authority over all things, observing and calling others to observe all that He has commanded us, assured that He is with us always—also in our academic work—"to the very end of the age" (Matthew 28:20).

## Conclusion

Recently, in a paper titled "Is There Hope for Africa?" Joel Carpenter, of Calvin College, observed, "More converts alone will not make a difference in this suffering continent" (1998, p. 18). What is needed, he said, ". . . is the engagement of Christianity with aspects of traditional African outlooks and values. However, in many settings, Christian faith operates on one level, while some of the deep structures of traditional values remain untouched." Carpenter continues:

> Across the African continent, community development workers and social and political reform leaders stress that a deeper Christian conversion, which makes for a renewing of minds, as the Apostle Paul puts it, is the key to social, economic, and political progress in Africa. Says the Nigerian Christian community development leader, Sulaiman Jakonda, ". . . it is imperative that Christians are adequately taught and made aware of kingdom values . . . they need to be made aware of the development realities of their communities and shown the way they can become

effective agents of change in society." So in addition to the high-level leadership development work that theological study centers are doing, grassroots education about the full dimensions of the Gospel and the principles of the Kingdom of God are the great challenges of the African church today. (1998, p. 18)

It has been our purpose and intent in this keynote presentation to describe and promote precisely that kind of education. It is not an abstract kind of education. Rather, it is education that acknowledges the full dimensions of the Gospel and enunciates the principles of the universal Kingdom of God, seeking thereby to qualify the Christian community to provide the hope that is needed, not only in Africa, but also throughout the world.

May God use this conference to help us gain further understanding into the nature of a Christian worldview for scholarship. And, following this conference, may God also use us, moved by His Spirit and directed by His Word, to realize the purpose of Christian higher education, which, as we earlier noted, is to enable kingdom citizens to understand the creation, their place in it, and their calling to bring to expression the kingdom rule of Christ over all things.

**References**

Calvin, J. (1936). *The Institutes of the Christian Religion,* Philadelphia: Presbyterian Board of Christian Education.

Carpenter, J. (November 19, 1998). Is there hope for Africa? *The noon lecture series,* Calvin Association for Life-Long Learning, Grand Rapids, MI.

Fowler, S. (1980). *Issues in the Philosophy of Education.* Potchefstroom, RSA: Potchefstroom University for Christian Higher Education.

Heslam, P. (1998) *Creating a Christian worldview: Abraham Kuyper's lectures on Calvinism.* Grand Rapids, MI: Eerdmans.

Heie, H. (1996). *Conversations for Christian higher education.* Grand Rapids, MI: Calvin College.

Hoekema, D. (1996). *Conversations for Christian higher education.* Grand Rapids, MI: Calvin College.

Holmes, A. F. (1983). *Contours of a world view.* Grand Rapids, MI: Eerdmans.

Kuyper, A. (1943). *Calvinism: Six Stone Foundation lectures.* Grand Rapids, MI: Eerdmans.

Leffel, J. (1996). Our New Challenge: Postmodernism. In Dennis McCallum (Ed.), *The Death of Truth,* 31. Minneapolis, MN: Bethany House Publishers.

Maatman, R. (1998). Suggestion: Use a World-and-Life View in the Teaching of Chemistry. *Journal of Chemical Education,* 65(10):885.

Moyers, B. (1996). *Genesis: A living conversation.* New York, NY: Doubleday.

Niebuhr, R H. (1956). *Christ and Culture.* New York, NY: Harper Collins.

Noll, M A. (1994). *The Scandal of the Evangelical Mind.* Grand Rapids, MI: Eerdmans.

Olthuis, J. H. "On World Views," in *Stained Glass: Worldviews and social science,* eds. Paul A. Marshall, Sander Griffioen, and Richard Mouw (Lanham: University Press of America, 1989), 26–40.

Schrotenboer, P. G. ( 1965, August). *Integral Christian Scholarship.* American Scientific Affiliation Conference, The King's College, Briarcliff Manor, NY.

Soden, D. E. and Storm, K. H. (1996, June). How Firm a Foundation? Postmodernism and the multicultural agenda. *Christian Scholars Review,* XXV(4):444.

Spykman, G. (1985). *Spectacles: Biblical Perspectives on Christian Scholarship.* Potchefstroom, RSA: Potchefstroom University for Christian Education.

Suk, J. (1996, November 18). What it Means to be Reformed: Tending Your Worldview. *The Banner.*

Van der Walt, B. J. (1997). *Being Human in a Christian Perspective.* Potchefstroom, RSA: Potchefstroom University for Christian Higher Education.

Van Dyk, J. (1978, Winter). Christian Education: Have We Thrown the Key Away? *Christian education conference,* Eastern Christian High School, Paterson, N.J.

Vanderstelt, J. C. (1996). Church in Society. *Rediscovery of the church II.*

Walsh, B. J. and Middleton, R. J. (1984). *The Transforming Vision: Shaping a Christian world view.* Downers Grove, IL: InterVarsity Press.

Wells, D. F. (1993). *No place for truth: or whatever happened to evangelical theology?* Grand Rapids, MI: Eerdmans.

Wolters, A. M. (1985). *Creation regained: biblical basics for a reformational worldview.* Grand Rapids, MI: Eerdmans.

Wolterstorff, N. (1993). Can Scholarship and Christian Conviction Mix: A New Look at the Integration of Knowledge. In Harold Heie and Arthur F. Holmes, (Eds.) *Universitas: The case for a new Christian university.*

# Chapter Three

**To the Reader –**

As I suggest in the introduction to this address, I was honored but also surprised to receive an invitation to speak on the subject of "Education for the Kingdom of God: Christian Education in a Plural Society." As I reflect on the matter, I should not have been surprised. The invitation probably came because of my president's inaugural address "A Place for Dordt College?" given little more than a year before. That address contained paragraphs such as the following:

Further, it should be noted that the state, because it is to administer justice with respect to all social structures, has a responsibility in regard to the school. It must not dominate the school. Instead, it must recognize that the school is a school and that it is the task of the state to protect the school from external intrusion, safeguarding the school's right to determine its religious direction and to make decisions of an academic nature. The "religious confessional plurality of school systems within society must be granted structural standing before the law." (McCarthy, et al, 1981, p. 167)

In any case, early August 1984 found me travelling to a beautiful retreat center, Cret-Berard, near Lausanne, Switzerland. Before and during the conference, I had an opportunity to spend some time with Dr. Jan Dengerink and the board of the International Association for Reformed Faith and Action (IARFA). We enjoyed profitable discussions that helped to strengthen the relationship between IARFA and the International Association for the Promotion Christian Higher Education (IAPCHE) and also provided me with some important guidelines when I later served as the Executive Secretary of IAPCHE.

Profitable discussions also took place during the conference in response to the various addresses and papers that were presented. Some of these discussions took interesting and unexpected turns. This was also the case with the responses to my address, in which I took the position that it is only in a truly pluralistic society that a Christian school, i.e., an institution of Christian education, can function effectively in educating people for the kingdom of God. I based this assertion on the principle of "sphere sovereignty" that rejects both "church absolutism" and "state absolutism" and honors the sovereignty of each sphere in fulfilling its task assigned by God who alone has the exclusive right to absolute sovereignty. Further, according to the principle of sphere sovereignty,

I argued that schools—along with other agencies in other spheres—must be allowed to function according to the requirements of structural and confessional pluralism.

It was while discussing structural and confessional pluralism that the discussion took an interesting turn. I don't recall exactly how or why this happened, but someone raised a question about homosexuality and suggested that it was the responsibility of the Christian community to press government to outlaw homosexuality. Recognizing that this position reflected a theonomistic position, I tried to point out that this position ran contrary to the concept of pluralism that the IARFA Conference was seeking to promote. I was helped in this by Professor Elaine Botha, from Potchefstroom University for Christian High Education (later called NorthWest University), who chaired the meeting and directed the discussion back to the main topic rather than continuing to discuss an issue that could have consumed most of the remaining time.

# Education for the Kingdom of God: Christian Education in a Plural Society

I want to begin this presentation by thanking you for giving me the opportunity to address a conference concerned with "Education for the Kingdom of God." I am directly involved in education for the kingdom of God; I believe that Christian education is essential to the ongoing progress of the kingdom of God, and I am pleased with the opportunity to come to this place to talk to others—who share this belief—about what is important in education for the kingdom of God.

The topic assigned to me is "Christian Education in a Plural Society." The letter of invitation added this word of explanation: "With plural we mean the fact that education has to be developed in a variety of social structures, as well as the fact that our society is plural in a religious sense." As we proceed, I trust you will note that I have attempted to do precisely what this word suggests.

At the same time, I want to make clear that I did not accept this assignment because I regard myself as an expert on the matter of social pluralism. In fact, at one point I suggested to the committee in charge that I should decline this invitation because of my busy schedule and the amount of work I knew would be involved in preparing this paper. When finally I did agree to accept the assignment, it was because I believe this issue is of tremendous importance to education for the kingdom of God. As far as I am concerned, "Christian Education in a Plural Society" is not an abstract topic. On the contrary, it concerns the continuing existence and well-being of our several institutions of Christian education.

Why do I say that "Christian Education in a Plural Society" concerns the existence and well-being of our institutions of Christian education? Because—and this is the central thesis of this paper—I believe it is only in a truly pluralistic society that a Christian school can function *effectively* in educating people for the kingdom of God.

To say that a Christian school can function *effectively* only in a plu-

---

Congress of the International Association for Reformed Faith and Action, August 4, 1984, Cret-Berard, Switzerland.

ralistic society is to insist that it cannot do so in a society that is dominated either by individualism or collectivism.

**Individualism and Collectivism**

*Individualism* insists that the individual is self-sufficient and precedes any and all societal relationships. This was the position of Thomas Hobbes, for example, who held that societal relationships are simply the result of a social contract consummated by a group of individuals (Spier, 1954, p 189).

It is not difficult to describe the implications of individualism for society, the state, or the schools (McCarthy et al, 1981, pp. 15–16). For individualists, the fundamental unit of society is the individual. Social institutions are merely names given to associations of individuals, who join together because they share common goals. They are artificial entities, which are to be held suspect because they constitute a threat to individual autonomy. Even the state is nothing more than an artificial creation of individuals acting together out of self-interest. It is the task of the state to protect the rights of individuals. When a state no longer performs its task, individual citizens have a right to eradicate it and to create a new one. In this view, the school is the result of private initiative, and it exists to provide educational services for the individual parent or student. The school is expected to be sensitive to the uniqueness of each child, seeking to develop individual gifts and talents.

There are, no doubt, elements of truth in individualism. Individuals are important; but they are not all-important. When individualism insists that individuals are self-sufficient, it makes the social character of human life an afterthought. It fails to recognize the social aspect of human life and the basic unity of the human race.

Individualism is unable to give an adequate account of the social institution called the state: "It does not have an eye for the unique and extensive task of state government by reason of its peculiar calling in society" (Dengerink, 1978, p. 19). Individualism, as propounded by John Locke, holds a basically negative view of the state. It holds that the state may not do anything that inhibits free individuals; but it does very little to clarify the meaning, purpose, and calling of the state.

Individualism also neglects the social aspects of the school and its task. This is evident, for example, in the writing of William James who has made a tremendous impact upon American thinking about education. According to Merle Curti:

> James was concerned primarily with the effect of habits upon the indi-

vidual rather than upon the social order. It has been pointed out that nowhere in *Talks to Teachers* does he speak of education as a social function. Maintaining that the basis of all education is the fund of native reactions with which the child is endowed, emphasizing interest as the motive power of all educational progress, and instinct as the beginning of interest, James conceived of education as the organization of acquired habits on the part of the individual in such a way as to promote his personal well-being. (1959, p. 448)

In this view the school becomes child-centered rather than society-centered. The purpose of the school is seen to be the training of free individuals for the social environment through the development of personal habits of virtue and morality. In the process the school also serves to give scientific support to individualism at the expense of social values.

In bold contrast to individualism, *collectivism* elevates one of the relationships of society above all others and considers that relationship to be an all-embracing totality, which includes lower relationships as its dependent parts. This is what Georg Hegel attempted, for example, with the *Ueberperson* of the state (Spier, 1954, p. 188).

As in the case of individualism, it is not difficult to set forth the implications of collectivism for society, the state, or the schools (McCarthy et al, 1981, pp. 17–18). Collectivism promotes a holistic view of society, with the collectivity as the primary unit of society. Only the collectivity possesses basic rights, and it is only within the collectivity that individuals and subgroups can find meaning and purpose. For most modern collectivists other institutions and organizations are absorbed into the dominant institution of the state. The state is all-powerful and sovereign. Other institutions exist primarily to serve the purposes of the state. One such institution is the school. (Historically the school has been controlled sometimes by the church and sometimes by the state. Modern collectivism usually views the state as predominant.) Schools are to be owned, funded, and operated by the state. Through the schools, the state is able to create the kind of community necessary for the operation of the state.

There are also elements of truth in collectivism. There can be no doubt that a sense of unity and solidarity is necessary for the efficient functioning of the society. But collectivism errs in seeking that unity by elevating one social institution above all others. To do so is to absolutize that institution—something that may not be done because no human institution, including the church or the state, should be viewed as the ultimate unit of society.

As we have already indicated, modern collectivism tends to envelop all other institutions within the dominant institution of the state. When this is done the distinction between state and society is inevitably erased, and the identity of the diverse social structures within society is obscured. Collectivism, as propounded by Jean Jacques Rousseau, "emerges with an idea of the state as embracing human life in its entirety" (Dengerink, 1978, p. 20). The state is universal, and it cannot tolerate any single particular institution beside it.

It must be observed that there have also been educational leaders who have been enthusiastic spokesmen for collectivism. Such a leader was William T. Harris, who was an adherent of Hegelian philosophy. One of the chief builders of the American public school system, Harris insisted that the national state was the most important of institutions. He declared that the public school system existed solely to train children for the state. From the collectivist viewpoint, therefore, the school loses its identity as a distinct institution within society. It is absorbed within the state and made to serve the purposes of the state.

It is important to note that individualism and collectivism tend to converge. This should not surprise us, since both find a common source in the Enlightenment philosophy of the French Revolution.

The tendency toward convergence can be seen in the thought of Thomas Jefferson, who reflected a "theoretical commitment to individualism and a pragmatic bent toward collectivism" (McCarthy et al, 1981, p. 84). This aspect of Jefferson's thought is important to our study because it produced a tension that became especially clear in his attitude toward public education:

> On the one hand Jefferson believed that individuals must constantly guard against surrendering their freedom to the state and that an educated citizenry was the best and most effective curb on government. On the other hand he willingly gave to the government the power to educate citizens in a given perspective. (McCarthy et al, 1981 p. 84)

This is a tension that constituted the beginnings of the contemporary argument that there should be a separation between public non-sectarian and private sectarian institutions, with the public school serving as a means for securing a stable social order.

In any case, the point is not to seek a middle road between individualism and collectivism. Instead, we must recognize that neither individualism nor collectivism acknowledges "the inner structure of societal relationships" (Spier, 1954, p. 189). Individualism denies the reality of societal relationships and considers them to be simply the names of arbitrary unions between sovereign individuals. Failing to recognize the social aspect of human life, individualism obviously will not result in a social situation in which the Christian school can function effectively in educating young people for that society that we call the kingdom of God. On the other hand, collectivism misconstrues the internal structural differences of societal relationships by insisting that it can comprehend human society in a scheme that would relate the whole to its parts by absolutizing the highest relationship—usually the state—as the total relationship. Such a perspective is contrary to the biblical view of the kingdom that recognizes only God as sovereign over all and, therefore, allows no aspect of the created order to be absolutized. Furthermore, collectivism would make the social institution of the school a means to prepare you people for the state, not for the kingdom of God.

We turn, therefore, to the alternative to individualism and collectivism, namely, *pluralism*.

**Varieties of Pluralism**

The term "pluralism" has a wide variety of meanings. According to Philip Wogaman, "The term 'pluralism' has, in fact, been invoked so routinely in current discussions as to risk becoming a mere cliché" (1967, p. 54).

In *The Pluralist Dilemma in Education*, Brian M. Bullivant speaks of pluralism on a cultural level or in cultural terms. The essence of the dilemma is stated in terms of this question: "How best to reconcile the legitimate claims of the nation-state with those of citizens who are from different social, economic, and cultural backgrounds?" (Bullivant, 1981, p. 1). Bullivant then point outs that the debate around this question has focused on education, because the schools must produce both individuals and citizens for the state—a reminder of the individualism-collectivism struggle.

David Nicholls, in *Three Varieties of Pluralism* (1974), identifies three ways in which social and political theorists have worked with a pluralist concept, i.e., English, American, and colonial models of pluralism. Both English and American pluralists, according to Nicholls, speak of groups and associations in society. The English see in groups—defined in a non-individualistic way—a defense of liberty over-against the dangers of an all-powerful state. Whereas contemporary American pluralists think primarily in terms of interest groups—defined in an individualistic way—and see government as maintaining an equilibrium between these groups, each attempting to gain some special position and advantage.

In Roman Catholic circles, pluralism has been defined largely in terms of sphere subsidiarity. And on the basis of this principle, Roman Catholics in America have done much to resist "the majoritarian notion of a single locus of educational authority" (McCarthy et al, 1981, p. 34). However, when viewed in its Thomistic context, sphere subsidiarity is, in reality, a form of shared collectivism. Church and state are each viewed as collectivist institutions, each in its own sphere—the church in the sphere of the supernatural and the state in the sphere of the natural.

When applied to the matter of education, sphere subsidiarity produces positions or statements such as the following:

> God and nature have given parents the right and duty to develop their children to full maturity. Unable to fulfill this duty unaided, parents use the agencies of society to assist them as authorized delegates. Chief among such agencies are the church and the state. Nonetheless, both the church and the state have other bases for their rights and duties in education. The church is commissioned to teach and to nourish the souls of men. The state is required not only to encourage and protect the rights and duties of the church and the family, and foster their fulfillment, but also to provide the forms of education necessary for political, military, and other citizenship requirements. From these rights and duties flow many roles and functions, which are to be performed both within and outside of the classroom. (Britt, 1966, p. 40)

There is no doubt that sphere subsidiarity provides an alternative to individualism and collectivism; but it leaves a number of important questions unresolved:

> Thus in the realm of the natural the state has the right to operate secular schools, while in the realm of the supernatural the church has an equally legitimate right to operate religious schools. Thus this view of society, the state, and the schools is in fact little more than a shared collectivism, which divides the collectivist jurisdiction between the natural and the supernatural, the state and the church. Some families are free to send their children to public schools under state control, while others have a similar freedom with respect to nonpublic schools under church control. But the question remains whether the identity and integrity of the home, the school, the other social institutions can be maintained without rendering them subsidiary to either the church or the state. (McCarthy et al, 1981, pp. 35–36)

The Calvinist tradition presents another version of pluralism that, in contrast to Roman Catholic sphere subsidiarity, speaks of *sphere sovereignty*. Sphere sovereignty means that no social sphere is subsidiary to any other sphere; but each sphere (state, church, family, school) functions with a sovereignty of its own—a sovereignty derived, of course, from

God. This Calvinist view results in a type of pluralism that, I believe, most effectively allows the school to function in educating young people for the Kingdom of God. And I will be concerned next to demonstrate that this is so.

## The History of Sphere Sovereignty

In the sixteenth century, the church was seen as essentially supranatural, as an addition to natural life. The state, on the other hand, was viewed as natural and as universalistically encompassing all other communities and associations. All societal relationships, with the exception of the church, were subjected to the totalitarian state; they derived their limited authorities and roles from the state.

This view of the state was accepted by Christians and incorporated into their world-and-life-view, even though it created a profound conflict of loyalties. How could they live with a totalitarian state and, at the same time, acknowledge and submit themselves to the universal claims of Jesus Christ? In the end, it was understood that these loyalties were mutually exclusive. The totalitarian state, into which all societal life was incorporated, was declared natural and outside the claims of Jesus Christ. The only place where the rule of Christ and His Word could be acknowledged was the institutional church, which was seen as an unnatural, supernatural addition to society, i.e., to the state.

As a result of the Reformation, and especially the views of John Calvin (1509–1564), a new perspective on the relationship of the church and state was provided. The central unifying theme that runs through all of the teaching and writing of Calvin is that of the over-arching, all-pervading *sovereignty of God.*

In light of his commitment to the absolute sovereignty of God, Calvin reinterpreted the church and state relationship. He could no longer limit the rule of Christ to the instituted church or ascribe to the church a place outside of the natural world. Nor could he allow the state to exist as a universalistic totalitarian and natural entity of, by, and for itself. According to Calvin, ultimate authority does not reside in the church or the state, "but in the will of the Lord who called both into existence" (Vanderstelt, 1969, p. 2). Only God's regime is total. Both "church absolutism" and "state absolutism" must be opposed as forms of idolatry which dishonor God's exclusive right to absolute sovereignty" (Spykman, 1976, p. 189).

> State and church are not really realms anymore but independent spheres with their own God-given laws.... Now it is no more a question of which

one of the two is more important, for both are of equal value insofar that both are subject to the ordinances of God. (Vanderstelt, 1969, p. 2)

In taking this position, Calvin implicitly "opens the door to the development of the principle of sphere sovereignty" (Spykman, 1976, p. 189).

The next challenge to the theory of state absolutism came from Johannes Althusius (1557–1638), a Calvinistic philosopher of law in Herborn, The Netherlands. Althusius took the principles of John Calvin and developed them into a social philosophy. He was careful to point out that the authority of God is not mediated through the church or the state. It comes directly so that each relationship or association exercises its own sovereignty in keeping with its own nature. This holds not only for the church and the state, but also for other associations such as families, guilds, and schools. Each has its own calling within the "symbiosis" (the living together within society). Further, each association has its proper laws by which it is ruled and these laws differ "in each species of association according as the nature of each requires" (Althusius, 1964, p. 16).

For the next two hundred years, the spirit of Rationalism and the Enlightenment—with its individualistic emphasis—dominated the Western world. Placing the individual at the center of society, enlightenment thinking devalued established norms and orders for societal life. Friederick Julius Stahl (1802–1855) of Germany was the first—following Althusius—to sense something of the principle of sphere sovereignty. Under the influence of the Reveil movement, Stahl came to see that government is bound to God's law for society and that church, marriage, and the state are independent spheres within society.

Stahl greatly influenced the thinking of Guilliaume Groen van Prinsterer (1801–1876), Archivist of the Royal House of Orange in The Netherlands. Groen, who was the first to use the phrase *"souvereiniteit in eigen sfeer"* (sovereign within its own sphere), viewed the state not as an all-encompassing community, but as an institution that is unique in that it is to promote the common welfare (Dooyeweerd, 1979, p. 53). At the same time Groen saw clearly the basic difference between the state, the church, and the family; he insisted that the state was not to interfere with the internal life of other spheres (Dooyeweerd, 1979, p. 54).

The clarity of this insight, however, was obscured by another perspective. Under the influence of the Historical School of thought, Groen was led to accept

> ... a view of society in which the independence of the various "spheres," with the important exception of the church-institute, is conceived as an autonomy, within the totality of the State, of subordinate parts that

have acquired rights of existence in the course of historical development. (Runner, 1967, p. 154)

Even though he did compromise his worldview with that of the Historical School, Groen, because he had gained a penetrating insight into the spiritual roots of his society, was instrumental in establishing a Christian day-school in Amsterdam in 1841. In fact, he is called "the father of the Christian school movement." He also struggled for forty years to organize a Christian political party in opposition to the liberalism of his day (Vanderstelt, 1969, p. 5).

The man who followed Groen van Prinsterer in The Netherlands was Abraham Kuyper (1837–1920). As a member of the Parliament, and subsequently as Prime Minister, Kuyper wanted to engage in political activity according to principles. This desire brought him face-to-face with questions about the nature and structure of society. He answered these questions in terms of the principle of sphere sovereignty.

In Kuyper's view, the Creator had submitted all creatures and societal relationships to His law. All of these societal entities must perform their tasks in terms of the peculiar authority delegated to them by God. In his address "*Souvereiniteit in Eigen Kring*" at the opening of the Free University of Amsterdam in 1880, Kuyper made clear that the various spheres in society—church, state, university, etc.—must be free from domination by other spheres in order that each might answer to its God-given task. Kuyper was especially concerned to make this clear relative to academic and scientific activity:

> Science also creates its own life sphere, in which Truth is Sovereign, and under no circumstances may violation of its life law be tolerated. To do so would not only dishonor science, but would also be sin before God. (Kuyper, 1880, p. 7)

In distinction from others before him, Kuyper saw sphere sovereignty as a creation principle, rather than being dependent upon an historical outlook. Out of this position he opposed humanism, which looks at society in terms of society itself, and Roman Catholicism with its dualistic worldview. In this way he also sought a pluralistic alternative to both individualism and collectivism.

In our century, the principle of sphere sovereignty has received philosophical correction and elaboration in the work of Herman Dooyeweerd (1894–1977), who was a professor in the juridical faculty of the Free University of Amsterdam. Dooyeweerd applied sphere sovereignty not only to societal relationships, but to all of created reality:

... "social facts" have not an existence in themselves, but only in the framework of permanent structures, in the sense of norm-laws, which are based on the order of Creation, as established by God. In the framework of these structures alone they are accessible for sociological thinking as well. (Dengerink, 1948, p. 264)

By means of the philosophy of "the cosmonomic idea," Dooyeweerd traced the theory of the sphere sovereignty of the social structures back, and rooted it in the diversity of the possibilities of human experience. This he called "the sphere sovereignty of the law spheres" (Klapwijk, 1980, p. 15).

## The Meaning of Sphere Sovereignty

The principle of *sphere sovereignty* stands at the center of a Reformed world-and-life-view, which seeks to explain the fullness of life in God's world from a biblical perspective. This *weltanschauung* (worldview) is based upon the writings of the Old and New Testaments, which are the "spectacles" through which all of creation is to be viewed. They enable us to see the laws that God has structured for His creation and to understand that, even though these structures have fallen under sin, God redeems and continues to uphold them through Jesus Christ—that is to say that redemption involves the restoration of the entire creation.

Out of this perspective comes the conviction that life as a whole is "religion," i.e., life is a response, obedient or disobedient, to God's sovereignty over all of the life of mankind. Thus Evan Runner writes:

> The concept of sphere sovereignty gives accurate expression to the scriptural revelation about the structural "bouw" or make-up of created reality and that it thus becomes, as the meaning of the divine word-revelation, our Arché, the Principle or Starting-point which drives, directs and governs all our life-activities in the world. (Runner, 1967, p. 133)

According to the Scriptures, in the beginning God created the world in an orderly fashion. The world was a cosmos, rather than a chaos, characterized by order, pattern, and structure, e.g., the things in creation that multiplied, multiplied "each according to its kind" (Genesis 1:24, 25). God also established the laws that were to govern the creation (Psalm 119:89–91) and gave each part its own nature and task. He subjected each part of creation, including societal life, to His law so that the various parts of creation might serve Him (Kalsbeek, 1975, p. 92). Thus the structures of creation and the rich diversity of these structures find their origin in the sovereign will of God and in the God-given creation order.

God also created man subject to the ordinances for His creation

(Genesis 1:27). But, in distinction from the rest of creation, "God created man in his own image" and mandated him to serve God by developing the potentialities of creation according to God's laws (Genesis 1:27–28). In this way mankind and the rest of creation was to serve God and show forth His glory. Failing in this assignment, mankind "exchanged the truth of God for a lie, and worshipped and served the created things rather than the Creator" (Romans 1:25).

But, through the death and resurrection of Jesus Christ, God redeemed His people and restored creation as the arena where He, once again, would be served and glorified (Colossians 1:19–22). As reward for His redemptive work, Christ was appointed by the Father as sovereign over all. Christ was given sovereign authority over all things (Matthew 28:18, Ephesians 2:14–15) and, by virtue of that authority, He commanded the new humanity, the Church, to work in the renewed creation according to His law and unto His praise (Matthew 28:19–20).

Mankind has an office, given by God to rule or administer the creation in obedience to the law of the Creator (Genesis 1:28). The creation belongs to God (Psalm 24:1–2), but mankind is to have dominion over creation as representative, steward, vice-gerent of God (Psalm 8:3–9). Thus mankind is not only given an office or a task to perform, but also a "particular right to perform it" (Runner, 1967, p. 146). Mankind is directly authorized by God for the pursuance of this task, and, in that sense, is given a "sovereignty" over creation; however, it is a delegated sovereignty and always subservient to the absolute sovereignty of God. By virtue of this commission from God, mankind is given "the right to act sovereignly in the name of the Sovereign" (Runner, 1976, p. 146).

In fulfilling this office before God, an individual is not to work in isolation but in relationship with others as part of the human community (Van Riessen, 1952, p. 79). And just as they structure other parts of creation, the laws of God structure human societal life, i.e., relationships with fellow human beings. It must not be supposed, however, that these human societal relationships—and the laws governing them—are vague and indefinite. They are relationships in which mankind is to work in the development of the creation order; and the structure that each relationship reflects is dependent upon the task to be performed within that relationship.

Initially, the human community was undifferentiated, and many spheres that we now recognize as such were originally subsumed under the family. But, in the course of history, as mankind performed the task of developing and unfolding the creation, differentiation occurred (Van

Riessen, 1952, p. 75). Different associations of society developed, according to the creational laws of God, associations that were distinct and independent according to their respective natures and functions. Thus there is today

> ... a wide variety of distinct, though related spheres which arise out of the complex life of mankind, each having its own task to perform, its own mandate entrusted to it by God. Thus there exists the sphere of the family, the sphere of science, of art, of technique and invention, of the church, and, to mention no more, the sphere of things which belong to Society as a whole. (Meeter, 1939, p. 159)

And within each of these spheres, we find a human community working with a particular aspect of the created order. In fact, it was through the exercise of particular offices and the performance of particular tasks that the different spheres were given form. This does not mean that the spheres within society are human creations. They are all based upon and reflections of the ordinances of God; but they were given historical formation through the instrumentality of the human community filling a particular office.

While it is true that the sovereignty that characterizes the various life spheres should not be viewed as preempting the sovereignty of God, the spheres do have a certain "sovereignty" in relationship to each other. Each sphere has its own identity and its own God-given structure in terms of which it is to function. Therefore each sphere has its own type of authority. Those who have authority in one sphere should not presume to have authority in other spheres. Everything in human society is interrelated; still each sphere has a type of authority that is distinctive in itself and must be honored by other spheres (Bouma, 1951, p. 27). The authority of one sphere is not derived from the authority of another. All authority is from God, who alone is sovereign. Thus, instead of the lower being subordinated to the higher, all spheres are subordinated to God and exist in a coordinate relationship to one another within the totality of the created order. Therefore,

> Sovereignty ... carries also the meaning of coordinate sovereignties. No delegated and limited sovereignty is subordinated to any other; each delegation of authority is directly from Christ. Thus, for instance, the husband's authority is not derived from the State of which he is a citizen or subject, but from Christ Himself. (Runner, 1967, p. 148)

Thus as mankind communally performed its God-given task, various independent, limited, and coordinate spheres developed, producing the social machinery that characterizes our highly organized society:

> ... from the task to maintain justice and order in public life the state has evolved. For the task of propagation and enriching human life by love, God instituted the family. In order to engage in worship and proclaim the message of salvation the church was formed. In order to transmit the culture of one generation to the next the school was instituted. In order to produce goods for human use industry and labor as distinct life zones came into being. (Schrotenboer, 1972, p. 18)

Closely related to the principle of sphere sovereignty is the principle of *sphere universality*. Sphere universality asserts the enkaptic interwovenness of societal spheres. It is the principle that all of the spheres are intimately connected in an unbreakable coherence. Just as sphere sovereignty stresses the distinctiveness of the social spheres, so sphere universality emphasizes their interrelatedness. As the Dordt College Study Report on Sphere Sovereignty states:

> Education, for instance, is closely interwoven with the state, for it is the latter's responsibility in our culture to set educational standards in order to ensure responsible citizens. This does not give the state authority to operate schools, however. Similarly, church and family are closely interwoven in a variety of ways; a fact, however, which does not give the church the right to dictate to parents the precise method in which they ought to raise their children. (Dordt College, 1974, p. 7)

Further, according to the principle of sphere universality, the spheres are not only closely related, but each sphere also mirrors all other spheres (Dooyeweerd, 1979, pp. 44–47). This is true, for example, of the sphere of the church. The church, which is to perform the task of preaching the gospel, reflects the sphere of the family as parents and children gather for worship; it reflects the sphere of education as it teaches the faith; it reflects the sphere of government as it regulates the affairs of the church, etc. In this way all the social spheres are integrally related to and with one another.

Earlier it was stated that observing the principle of sphere sovereignty avoids the extremes of collectivism and individualism. Kalsbeek makes the same point regarding sphere universality by stating that two false conclusions arise when we lose sight of this principle:

> The first is a universalistic view of society. Sociological universalism, however consistent or inconsistent it may be, always constructs a temporal societal whole of which all other societal spheres are but organic parts. The other conclusion is the exact opposite: an individualistic view of society. Those who follow this line of thought say that society is a whole which has arisen from the relations between separate individuals. (Kalsbeek, 1975, p. 202)

Which lead us, finally, to consider:

### The Calvinist Concept of Sphere Sovereignty

Out of this Calvinistic tradition—which speaks both of sphere sovereignty and sphere universality—comes a type of pluralism which, according to H. Henry Meeter,

> . . . is not determined by mere practical considerations out of a bias in favor of either Church or State, or a preference for individualism or collectivism. The Calvinist considers all lawful organizations, whether Church or State or organic associations in Society, as God-established, and, therefore, deserving of their due rights. (1939, pp. 158, 159)

This Calvinist perspective includes two basic dimensions: structural pluralism and confessional pluralism.

*Structural pluralism* sees pluralism as reflecting the ordered structures of creation. There is a unity in creation; the creation is a cosmos, a harmonious whole. And, even as human life develops more complex and differentiated forms, this unity remains—as indicated in the principle of sphere universality. The creation, however, is not a seamless garment. There is also rich diversity in the creation. As human life historically unfolds, the various spheres of social activity show forth this diversity—as described in the principle of sphere sovereignty. Each sphere has its own function, its own area of jurisdiction. No sphere or association is to dominate another. This is structural pluralism.

The Calvinist tradition also includes *confessional pluralism,* which seeks to recognize society's "wide range of contrasting faith communities" (McCarthy et al., 1981, p. 39). These communities must be free to live according to their religious convictions and, at the same time, must enjoy equal protection by the law of the land, with liberty and justice for all.

And what are the implications of this type of pluralism?

Pluralism, from a Calvinistic perspective, holds that man is a social being. He cannot be reduced to an isolated individual or a unit within some social whole. The individuality of man finds meaning only within the framework of societal structures. On the other hand, no one societal structure can claim to be the place where ultimate meaning is located. However, multiple social structures—such as family, school, church, and state—do have meaning. Structural pluralism, therefore, recognizes a plurality of associations, each functioning in its own sphere. And confessional pluralism acknowledges the right of various faith communities to function in each sphere in harmony with their religious commitment. No faith group is given a privileged status. The rights affirmed for one faith group are insisted upon for all.

The original mandate for the state was given in the creation order. The state is to administer public justice among all societal institutions and associations (Romans 13).

In order to understand what is meant by public justice we must be sensitive to the biblical idea of *office*. Man, as crown of God's creation, is called to be God's officer, God's steward in the creation. There is a wide variety of offices, such as parent, teacher, citizen, church member, worker, and magistrate. In its promotion of justice, the state must administer policy so as to preserve man's freedom in the fulfillment of these manifold offices or callings in society.

> The state functions as the balance wheel in society, balancing out as equitably as possible the conflicts of interest that arise among different institutions (structural pluralism) and among different faith communities (confessional pluralism). (McCarthy et al., 1981, p. 165)

Applying social justice relative to the social institution of the school means that the state must work for educational equity. Recognizing that the school is an educational institution, the school must be given the freedom to function in terms of its own structure and task, its own rights and sovereignty—according to the requirements of structural pluralism.

As Van Riessen indicates, in speaking concerning the spheres in general (1952, pp. 70–71), three laws must be recognized as applying to the school. First, there is the law of *independence*. The school has its own educational, academic nature, its own laws according to which it must operate, and its own task that it is to perform by virtue of the charge given it by God. Second, there is the law of *limitation*. Since the school has sovereign rights within its own domain, it may not seek to usurp or dominate another sphere. To do so would not only violate the independence of other spheres but would also usurp the power and authority of God. Third, there is the law of *coordination*. The school is not subordinate to the authority and control of other spheres. This is not to say that all spheres are of equal importance. According to the order of creation, there is an obvious difference in value among the spheres; but recognition of this difference does not imply a hierarchy. The authority of the school is not derived from other spheres, such as the family, state, or church. All authority is from God, who alone is sovereign. The school is subordinate to God alone and exists in a coordinate relationship to other spheres within the totality of society.

The authors of *Society, State, and Schools* present the state as holding a threefold relationship to the schools.

> First, the state must safeguard the right of all schools to freely determine their own religious commitments and philosophies of education—whether Roman Catholic, Lutheran, Amish, Hebrew, Baptist, Calvinistic, Secular, Atheist, or any other. Second, in pursuit of its task to execute public justice, the state must assure itself of the health, safety, good order, equitable treatment, and well-being of both the teaching staff and the student population in its various schools. Third, decisions on issues that are specifically academic belong rightfully to and should therefore be made, not by state officials, but by representatives of the academic community. (McCarthy et al., 1981, p. 167)

If the state carefully observes this relationship, it will concern itself only with the political dimensions of school life. At the same time the school will be free to concentrate on academic matters, such as curriculum, certification, student achievement, length of school terms, etc.

In addition, there are the requirements of confessional pluralism. The religious plurality of school systems must also be given equitable, evenhanded, and impartial standing before the law. Not only the school that agrees with the religious vision of a particular state, but all school systems must be given the right and the freedom to determine their confessional stance and to regulate their academic affairs accordingly. In this way, recognition is given to the legal right of each faith community—including the Christian school that is committed to training and educating young people for the kingdom of God—to work out its religious perspective in a structured program of education.

## Conclusion

A number of conclusions may be drawn from the material that I have set forth in this paper. I wish to mention only two conclusions that, it seems to me, are obvious and essential relative to the theme of this conference, "Education for the Kingdom of God."

First, as members of the Reformed Christian community, we must employ all legitimate means to press for the plural society that we have described as being required by our Calvinistic tradition. We share the conviction that Christ-centered education is required, commanded by our Lord. That being the case, we not only may but we must do whatever we can to work in our respective countries for that plural society that allows us along with others the freedom, without hindrance, to train young people by means of Christ-centered education for the kingdom of God.

Second, while pressing for a pluralistic society, we must see to it that the educational enterprise where we are engaged is and continues to be truly Christian. The pluralistic society we seek is based upon the sovereignty of God over all of life. It is only when we recognize God's sovereignty—also in scholarship and teaching—that we have the right and duty before God to seek that freedom to educate for the kingdom of God that a truly plural society affords us.

**References**

Althusius, J. (1964). *Politics*. (trans. F. S. Carney), London: Eyre and Spottiswoode.

Bouma, C. (1951). The relevance of Calvinism for today. In Calvinistic Action Committee, *God-centered living*. Grand Rapids, MI: Baker.

Britt, J. F. (1966). Rights and Roles of Parents, Church, and State in Education. In Daniel D. McGarry and Leo Ward (Eds.), *Educational freedom and the case for government aid to students in independent schools*. Milwaukee, WI: The Bruce Publishing Company.

Bullivant, B. M. (1981). *The pluralist dilemma in education*. London: George Allen and Unwin.

Curti, M. (1959). *The social ideas of American educators*. Tatowa, NJ: Adams and Company.

Dengerink, J. (1948). *Critisch-historisch onderzoek naar de sociologische ontwikkeling van het beginsel der "sovereiniteit in eigen kring" in de 19e and 20e eeuw*. Kampen, NLD: J.H. Kok.

Dengerink, J. (1978). *The idea of justice in Christian perspective*. Toronto: Wedge Publishing Foundation.

Dooyeweerd, H. (1979). *Roots of western culture*. (trans. John Kraay) Mark Vander Vennen and Bernard Zylstra (Eds.) Toronto: Wedge Publishing Foundation.

Dordt College. (1974). Study Report on Sphere Sovereignty. Sioux Center, IA: Dordt College.

Kalsbeek, L. (1975). *Contours of a Christian philosophy*. (trans. Judy Peterson) Mark Vander Vennen and Bernard Zylstra (Eds.), Toronto: Wedge Publishing Foundation.

Klapwijk, J. (1980, 30, No. 2). The struggle for a Christian philosophy: Another look at Dooyeweerd. *Reformed Journal*.

Kuyper, A. (October 20, 1880). *Sphere sovereignty*. (trans. George Kamps) Amsterdam, NLD: Inauguration of the Free University.

McCarthy, R et al. (1981). *Society, state, and schools*. Grand Rapids, MI: Eerdmans.

Meeter, H. H. (1939). *Calvinism: an interpretation of its basic ideas*. Grand Rapids, MI: Zondervan.

Nicholls, D. (1974). *Three varieties of pluralism*. New York, NY: St. Martin's Press.

Runner, H. E. (1967). *The relation of the Bible to learning*. Rexdale, ON: The Association for Reformed Scientific Studies.

Schrotenboer, P. (1972). *Man in God's world*. Toronto, ON: Wedge Publishing

Foundation.

Spier, J. M. (1954). *An introduction to Christian philosophy.* (trans. David Hugh Freeman) Philadelphia, PA: The Presbyterian and Reformed Publishing Company.

Spykman, G. (1976). Sphere-Sovereignty in Calvin and the Calvinistic Tradition. In David Holwerda (Ed.), *Explaining the heritage of John Calvin.* Grand Rapids, MI: Baker.

Van Riessen, H. (1952). *The Society of the Future.* (trans. David H. Freeman) Philadelphia, PA: The Presbyterian and Reformed Publishing Company.

Vanderstelt, J. (August, 1969). Christian Action and Sphere Sovereignty, Conference of the Christian Action Foundation. Sioux Center, IA: Dordt College.

Wogaman, P. (1967). *Protestant faith and religious liberty: The basis of religious freedom in protestant theology.* Nashville, TN: Abingdon Press.

# Chapter Four

**To the Reader-**

When asked by Dordt's Natural Science Department to speak to the Science Symposium, I was quite new to the Dordt community. Early in its history, I had been involved in promoting the college and had also participated in the conversation around the development of its Statement of Purpose. But I had not become a member of the faculty until 1968, when I accepted the appointment to serve as Campus Pastor and to teach courses in Biblical Theology.

So, when the invitation came to speak on "The Relation Between the Bible and Science," I felt challenged to produce a presentation that was worthy of academic consideration and that was in harmony with Dordt's reformational statement of purpose. From the beginning it had been clear that fundamental to the identity of Dordt "is the conviction that the Scriptures are the Word of God, revealing not only the way to salvation in Jesus Christ, but providing the key to the understanding, interpretation, meaning, and purpose of the whole cosmos." But how was that statement to be interpreted and applied in our research and teaching?

It became clear, as I discussed this question with various members of the Dordt community, that there was a variety of answers being given to this question. This led me to the conclusion that I was going to discuss rather than to give or provide the answer to the question—which is what I tried to do.

# THE RELATION BETWEEN THE BIBLE AND SCIENCE

It was several months ago that I was asked to prepare a paper on the subject, "What is the relation between the Bible and science?" Having accepted the request, I began seriously and somewhat confidently to prepare for the presentation of a meaningful answer to the question. It must not be supposed that I had never considered this matter before. But it is not often that someone who is a college pastor and Bible instructor has the opportunity or temerity to address a gathering such as this concerning so important an issue. Therefore, I looked upon this assignment as the occasion for a renewed consideration of and struggle with the matter at hand.

As I have already stated, this is not the first time I have considered this matter. In fact, I had lectured on this subject to a group of Christian educators just three months prior to receiving your request. But today I marvel at my audacity, and I must confess that much of my confidence has evaporated. As time permitted, I have been reading, discussing, inquiring, thinking, and praying about this matter. Just what is the relationship of the Bible to science? The more I inquired, the more confused and uncertain I became. Now if this were merely a personal problem, you may be certain I would not be troubling you with it. But it is becoming increasingly clear to me that confusion and uncertainty concerning this matter characterize the Christian academic, scientific community-at-large.

Permit me to cite an example of what I am talking about. In the December 1969 issue of the *Journal of the American Scientific Affiliation*, Bernard Ramm reports on a symposium concerning "The Relationship between the Bible and Science." I assume that all who participated in that symposium are qualified, capable scholars and, as Christians, acknowledge the Bible to be the inscripturated Word of God. But it must not be supposed that their qualifications and commitment to the Bible produced identical or even similar answers to the question posed. One con-

---

Dordt College Science Symposium, March, 1971.

tributor took the position that "there is no relationship between the Bible and science as we know it today." Another stated, "I regard the Bible and science as two complementary, essentially non-overlapping approaches to truth." Another wrote, "I feel that the Bible has very little to say about science in a general way, but that it has everything to say about the scientist." And still another insisted, "Wherein the Bible speaks of any aspect of science, it does so authoritatively and with reliability"(Ramm. 1969, pp. 97–124).

This variation of thought and conviction is found throughout the evangelical scientific community today. On the one hand, there is the position that tends to view the Bible as the infallible source of scientific data and information. On the other hand, there is the position that regards the Bible as revealing only that which has to do with man's salvation through faith in Jesus Christ, but as having nothing to say about the redeemed man's scholarly, scientific thought and activity. (The word *man* is used in this paper to mean "human being," whether male or female.) And, of course, there are varying shades of opinion between these two positions. I wish I could say that this division of thought is not found in the Reformed community. However, such is not the case. In spite of its rich heritage and frequent address to this question, the Reformed community as well as the rest of the evangelical world reflects a wide variety of thought and opinion on this matter.

Harry Van Der Laan, in *A Christian Appreciation of Physical Science*, points out that the same variation and conflict of opinion has existed relative to the "age-old problem of 'science and belief.'" He states: "This problem has been prominent since the time of the early Church Fathers, dominant especially since the Renaissance until the present day. The history of civilization, the history of the church, and the history of science reverberate with the echoes of this question and the multitude of answers provided as time unfolded" (1966, p. 14). He goes on to indicate that the outcome of the confrontation between "science and belief" has been: "Any of the following three: the two wage unrelenting war; the two exist in some accommodated relation; or the two exist totally apart in two separate worlds. The first and the last are extremes: we will characterize them as war and apartheid. As you would expect, the great crowd is found in the moderate wing, that of coexistence. We all know people of all camps, perhaps some of us feel at home in one or another" (1966, p. 15).

This situation should concern all of us. Not that Christians involved in scientific activity must agree on all matters; but the place of the Bible in scientific thought and activity is a fundamental issue. It concerns our use of and attitude toward that which is "God-breathed" and is "useful for teaching, rebuking, correcting and training in righteousness, so that the man of God may be thoroughly equipped for every good work" (2 Timothy 3:16, 17).

I would not be so presumptuous as to claim that I am about to give the final solution to our problem. But, I do hope to indicate where I believe we must begin if we are to come to a true and agreed understanding of this matter; which understanding, in turn, will give us a united Christian perspective for viewing and engaging in our scientific task.

It is my conviction that we must begin with a biblical view of man in relationship to God, to the creation, and to man's task within the creation. It is my conviction, further, that if we do begin with this biblical perspective, we are going to come to the conclusion that much of our problem results from asking the wrong question, or asking the question in the wrong way. For it seems to me that, when we inquire concerning the relationship between the Bible and science, we are viewing both the Bible and science as entities existing in abstraction. But they do not exist in abstraction. The Bible is God's Word addressed to man, and science is an activity that is performed by and is never separated from man. Are we trying to see the relationship between two things—the Bible and science—which are not and cannot be seen in relationship to one another apart from man and the heart of man? I think so. Permit me to try to explain what I mean.

The Bible begins with these words: "In the beginning God created the heavens and the earth" (Genesis 1:1). God is the Creator of all. God created all things by and for His Son (Colossians 1:15–17). As Creator, God is to be distinguished from His creation (Psalm 90:2), and yet the creation is always dependent upon God for its continuation and existence (Nehemiah 9:6). The creation is also subject to God, that is, it is His kingdom over which He is sovereign. The creation is the kingdom of God, not only because it belongs to Him (Psalm 24:1) but also and especially because He rules the creation and it is subject to His law or laws (Psalm 119:89–91).

God, the Creator, imposed laws upon His creation. Perhaps it would be more correct to say that He created according to these laws and that He continues to maintain them. The laws of God, whereby the creation is structured, apply to all of created reality. By virtue of these laws every aspect of creation is distinguished from every other aspect and yet is related to all other aspects (Wolthuis, 1965, p. 93). Thus there is diversity within the creation, each part or aspect distinguished by its own peculiar law. And yet there is unity in the creation. All the various laws of the creation are one in God through His Son in whom "all things hold together" (Colossians 1:17). Thus we may speak of God's creation as a cosmos, an ordered unit, interrelated in all its parts. It was and is God's purpose that the creation, in its diversity and unity, function harmoniously according to His law or laws, and thus fulfill its purpose to glorify Him of whom, through whom, and unto whom are all things (Romans 11:36).

Man is part of God's creation, and yet he occupies a unique place or position in creation. This is so because "God created man in his own image, in the image of God he created him, male and female he created them" (Genesis 1:27). By virtue of his creation in the image of God, man stood as the crown of creation in covenantal relationship to God. And through man—more particularly the heart of man—the whole creation was united to God. In this covenantal context, man received the Word of God. God spoke to man, to man's heart. God called man to love Him, to live with and for Him, and to work for Him in the creation. Thus God gave man(kind) a command, a mandate: ". . . and God said to them, Be fruitful and increase in number; fill the earth and subdue it. Rule over the fish of the sea and the birds of the air and over every living creature that moves on the ground" (Genesis 1:28). Thus, by means of His Word addressed to man's heart, God called man to subdue the creation in loving and humble obedience to Him. Thereby God would fulfill His purpose for creation through man.

Man received a calling, an office. What was that calling? The late Herman Hoeksema describes it beautifully in his *Reformed Dogmatics*:

> He therefore had a very definite task to perform. But in all his life and work he was to be busy as the friend-servant of God; not as a slave, who works from the motive of fear for the whip; not as a wage earner, who puts in his hours merely for his wages; but freely, from the love of God, as His co-worker; and being of His party, as the friend of God he was to function as God's superintendent over all the works of God's hands. As such he must replenish and subdue the earth, cultivate and keep the garden, and bring to light all the wonders and powers of the world. And the pure delight of it in the favor of God was his reward. (Hoeksema, 1966, p. 223)

In these words, Hoeksema describes what was to be man's response to the cultural mandate given by God.

In the performance of his cultural task, however, man must discover and understand the laws of God by which the creation was structured and according to which it was to function. Man had to distinguish the various aspects of creation and yet see them in their cosmic relationship. Further, man was to work with and in the creation according to the laws for creation. Living and searching and working in blessed fellowship with God according to His law, man was to bring glory and praise to the Creator.

In light of what has been said thus far, it is evident that there was to be a scientific aspect to man's cultural activity. Concerning culture, Van Der Laan writes:

> What about *culture*? We speak of culture, civilization, *beschaving*. It refers to man in his constructive activity, and the results of such activity. Men and their work, developed communally in historic and geographic relation, that is culture. Man's building, constructing, forming, it is free formation, so that "culture is a procession of new things." [Van Riessen, *The Society of the Future*.] Man is called upon to build and so to glorify God. This forming is the disclosure of what is enclosed in the creation. (1966, p. 24)

Van Der Laan then goes on to say, "Science, scholarship is part of culture" (1966, p. 24). And what is meant by science? Hendrik Van Riessen, in *The Christian Approach to Science* states: "Science aims at knowledge of reality" (1959, p. 12). More specifically, Van Der Laan writes: ". . . what is the aim, the immediate purpose of scientific inquiry? The most concise answer is: to acquire knowledge of law" (1996, p. 41). And further on, Van Der Laan states: "The aim of science is to acquire knowledge of structural laws" (1966, p. 42). Accepting these statements as descriptions of the nature and purpose of science as I do, it is clear that "science" is an aspect of the cultural task of man before God, it is an aspect whereby man is to seek to analytically discover and disclose the various laws of the creation.

At this juncture, we should make two observations relative to the main point of this paper. First, we must not view the Word of God as the abstract speech of God functioning apart from man. Rather, we must see the Word of God as the powerful address of God to man's heart, calling and directing man to work as God's loving, obedient servant in and with the creation. Nor should we see the cultural and the scientific as existing abstractly of and by themselves. Rather, they are activities of man in which man is to engage as a called and directed servant of God.

Second, and in connection with the above, it is important to note and remember that, from the beginning, the Word of God, addressed to man's heart, pointed man to and was intended to direct man in the performance of his God-given task. The Word of God, as such, did not make known to man the nature and function of the various laws of creation. The Word of God pointed man to his task and directed him in the performance of that task as servant of God in the creation of God. And it was for man, living in fellowship with God through the Word, to discover the laws of creation and to work with and according to those laws unto God's glory. Relative to the scientific aspect of man's task, this means that man was not to seek knowledge of creation's structural laws by contemplating the Word of God but by an analysis of these laws themselves and by performing this analysis as servant of God, called and directed by the Word of God addressed to his heart.

Through the disobedience of Adam, the bond of covenantal fellowship between God and man, and also between God and the creation through man, the crown of creation, was broken. Man remained man, the image-bearer of God, responsible to live in loving and obedient service to God. The creation remained a cosmos, functioning in its unity and diversity according to the laws of God. But, because of man's refusal to love and obey God, the entire creation came under the terrible influence of man's sin.

The effects of sin are seen most clearly relative to the heart of man. The heart, as E.L.H. Taylor writes in *The Christian Philosophy of Law, Politics, and the State*, "is the concentration point of our entire human existence . . . . The heart is the point where man decides his relationship with Almighty God. It can never be neutral. It loves God or it is hostile to him" (Taylor, 1966, p. 66). Out of man's heart "is the wellspring of life" (Proverbs 4:23). And so "As he thinketh in his heart, so is he" (Proverbs 23:7 KJV). Having fallen into sin, the heart of man turned from God. "The fool says in his heart, 'There is no God'" (Psalm 14:1). And, instead of fixing itself upon God the Creator, the heart of man turned to the creation itself. Man "exchanged the truth of God for a lie, and worshiped and served created things rather than the Creator—who is forever praised" (Romans 1:25). Man no longer worked as a loving servant of God, but as an enemy of God. Man no longer sought the glory of God, but "deified" and served himself or another aspect or part of the creation.

The effects of sin are also seen in the cultural activity of Cain and his descendants as they worked in and within God's creation (Genesis 4). They were culturally busy. (We may assume, further, that they were also scientifically active, although it is impossible to identify the scientific aspect of their cultural activity.) They built a city, erected houses, established homes, raised cattle, manufactured and played musical instruments, sang songs, produced weapons, and fought wars. You see? Man was yet man. The creation was yet a cosmos. Man was yet culturally active in the creation, but he worked as an enemy, not as an obedient servant, of God. Out of his evil heart he produced and brought forth evil, that is, that which was opposed to God (Luke 6:45). Worshipping and serving the creature rather than the Creator, man named his cities after himself; he used marriage for his own satisfaction; he fought wars to elevate himself; and he sang songs to his own glory.

But God was not about to allow His purposes to be thwarted by sinful man. Through His Son Jesus Christ, the Word of God become flesh; He performed the glorious and gracious work of redemption. By means of His redemptive work, Christ restored His people and, through them, the entire creation to covenantal fellowship with God:

> For God was pleased to have all his fullness dwell in him, and through him to reconcile to himself all things, whether things on earth or things in heaven, by making peace through his blood, shed on the cross. (Colossians 1:19–21)

Having accomplished His work, Christ ascended to the right hand of God and was there enthroned as the Head of His redeemed people, the Church, and as King of the redeemed creation, His kingdom. He was given all power in heaven and on earth (Matthew 28:18) so that, through the redeemed citizens of His kingdom, He might subdue the earth unto God's glory. This means, of course, that those who were enemies when Christ died for them, must become a people for God's own possession, that they may show forth the excellencies of Him who called them out of darkness into His marvelous light (1 Peter 2:9).

How do the "alienated" ones, the enemies of God, become friends and servants of God in God's world, His kingdom? They must be gripped by the Word of God, Jesus Christ Himself (John 1:1, 14). And how does this happen? Jesus Christ is revealed to man in the Bible, the inscripturated, divinely inspired, infallible Word of God. Jesus Himself, referring to the Scriptures, said, ". . . these are the Scriptures that testify about me" (John 5:39). Through the Bible and the working of His Spirit, Christ, the Word of God, addresses Himself to the heart of sinful man. And, doing so, He turns man in his heart so that man, through faith and repentance, surrenders to God as His loving and obedient servant.

By means of the Bible and the work of the Holy Spirit, therefore, man once again hears, is gripped, and is directed by the Word of God. He sees the awfulness of his sin and makes a confession. He sees himself restored through Christ's death and resurrection to his place as God's servant. He sees the creation as God's and as the arena in which he is to live and work as God's servant, according to God's law, and unto God's glory. Once again he stands before the mandate of God. He is to build, construct, and form—engage in cultural activity—for God, his Lord and Redeemer. He is to abstract, analyze, and synthesize—engage in scientific activity—unto the praise of His Maker and Savior. And as he does so he hears the assuring Word, ". . . surely I will be with you always, to the very end of the age" (Matthew 28:20).

I began this paper by stating that it is my conviction—in light of the biblical view of man in relationship to God, the creation, and man's task in the creation—that our problem concerning the Bible and science is due primarily to our asking the wrong question or asking the question in the wrong way. I hope that you can now appreciate why I made that statement.

Recall the observations made earlier relative to man's pre-fall situation and consider them now in the context of the post-fall, redemptive situation. First, it should be clear that we may not view the Bible, the inscripturated Word of God, as an abstract Word functioning apart from its address to the heart of man. Rather, we must read the Bible as the Word of God revealing Christ Jesus to man's heart, bringing him to redemption in Christ and directing him to work as God's loving, obedient servant, according to God's laws, in God's creation, and unto God's glory. It is evident, further, that we may not view the cultural and the scientific as existing abstractly apart from man and his heart. Rather, they must be seen as activities in which the redeemed man is to engage, called and directed by Scripture, as a servant of God.

Second, as we noted concerning the Word of God prior to man's fall into sin, it is important to note and to remember now that the Bible, revealing Christ to man's heart, points man to and directs him in the performance of his task. Man does not fulfill his cultural responsibility by simply studying and working with the Bible. Rather, the Bible, which he must read and study, points the redeemed man to his cultural work and directs him in that work as a servant of God in God's creation. And it is for the redeemed man, living in fellowship with God through Christ revealed in Scripture, to work culturally with and according to God's laws and unto His glory. Relative to the scientific aspect of man's task, this means that the redeemed, the Christian scientist is not to perform his task by engaging in a scientific analysis of the Bible (unless perhaps he is a theologian), but by carrying on his scientific work—abstracting, analyzing, synthesizing—as God's servant, directed by the Scriptures as they speak to his heart.

I do not mean to say that the Bible, in revealing the person Jesus Christ to the heart of the scientist, is without content that should be read and contemplated by the Christian scientist.

And I certainly do not intend to leave the impression that the Bible has nothing to say to the scientist about his scientific activity. But the Bible—and this has been said often—is not a scientific textbook; that is, it does not speak scientifically. It speaks to the heart of the redeemed scientist, qualifying and directing him in the performance of his scientific work as a servant of God. This, it seems to me, is what Paul is saying to Timothy in 2 Timothy 3:16–17: All Scripture is God-breathed and is useful for teaching, rebuking, correcting, and training in righteousness, so that the man of God may be thoroughly equipped for every good work." The work of the Christian scientist is that of theoretical abstraction and analysis. The Bible is profitable to teach, reprove, correct, and instruct the Christian scientist in righteousness so that he may do his scientific work as a servant of God.

Therefore, acknowledging science to be an activity of the redeemed man in which he is directed by the Scriptures, I would suggest that we rephrase the question and inquire as to what is the relationship between the Bible and the heart of the Christian scientist; and, further, how the Bible thus directs the Christian scientist in his scientific work. Perhaps from this perspective and asking these questions we can, with God's blessing, come to the agreed upon and united understanding that we seek.

## References

Hoeksema, H. (1966). *Reformed Dogmatics*. Grand Rapids, MI: Reformed Free Publishing Association.

Ramm, B. (December, 1969). *Journal of the American Scientific Affiliation*.

Taylor, E.L.H. (1966). *The Christian Philosophy of Law, Politics, and the State*. Nutley, N.J.: The Craig Press.

Van Riessen, H. (1959). *The Christian approach to Science*. Hamilton, ON: The Association for Reformed Scientific Studies.

Van Der Laan, H. (1966). *A Christian appreciation of physical science*. Hamilton, ON: The Association for Reformed Scientific Studies.

Wolthuis, E. (1965). *Science, God, and you*. Grand Rapids, MI: Baker.

# Chapter Five

**To the Reader –**
I've always considered it an honor to address the annual convention of the National Union of Christian Schools' Association of Christian School Administrators (ACSA), an association composed primarily of Christian school board members and administrators from throughout North America. The NUCS is now known as Christian Schools International (CSI). I was especially honored to be invited to speak to the 54th Annual Convention, held August 6–8, 1974, on the campus of York University in Toronto, Ontario. The convention theme was "Kaleidoscope of Christian Leadership," and my assigned topic was "Leadership in the Christian Community." In other words, I was being asked on this occasion to speak to leaders about leadership! Discussion after the speech indicated great interest in the topic.

The convention was soon followed by a request from the Ontario (Canada) Christian Schools Principals' Conference that I follow up on the convention address by speaking specifically about "Leadership in the Christian School." I responded positively to this invitation as I did to others from Christian school communities in South Korea, Australia, Africa, and the United States. This was obviously a topic the Christian school community throughout the world was grappling with.

I had given much thought to the subject of "leadership" while serving on the Purposes Committee of Dordt College. I was asked to chair a subcommittee assigned to deal with and report on "Authority in Christian Higher Education." This assignment resulted in a June 1973 *Pro Rege* article in which I dealt with the concept of "sphere sovereignty," observing that sphere sovereignty and authority are closely related subjects. Preparing for the 1974 NUCS Convention presentation on "leadership," I also came to the realization that "sphere sovereignty" is important to an understanding of "leadership" in the Christian community and especially in the Christian academic community.

As I now reflect on the time before and during my presidency of Dordt College (1982–1996), I recall that my writing and speaking about leadership in Christian education did much to prepare me for and guide me in my presidency. In 1976 I was given leave to begin doctoral studies at the Iliff School of Theology in Denver, Colorado. In 1981 I submitted my doctoral dissertation "The Role Identity of the Campus Pastor of a Church-Related Liberal Arts

College," in which I asserted in the closing sentence that "the Reformed principle of the sovereignty of the social spheres" guides us in understanding that role. In 1982, I was appointed president of the College. In my inaugural address I promised "to perform my work not as a master but as a servant leader" aiding the various sub-communities in the Dordt community—communities identified according to the principle of sphere-sovereignty.

The point? "Leadership in the Christian Community" not only reflected my point of view, but also had an impact upon my leadership at Dordt College and throughout the Christian academic community.

# Leadership in the Christian School

I've been travelling in Canada quite a bit lately, assisting the work of the Advancement Office of Dordt College. Doing so, I've been impressed with two things: 1) the growth and development of your program of Christian education, and 2) the seriousness with which you approach your educational tasks and responsibilities. For example, I recently spent two days in Edmonton. While there, I learned that the principal of the Christian high school is leaving his administrative post in order that he may spend more time working specifically on the articulation of a united curriculum. I find this most exciting and, at the same time, essential to the progress of the Christian academic enterprise.

I believe my task as your speaker today is quite well-defined in the following paragraph of the letter sent to me by the planning committee:

> We would like to have you prepare a 45 minute to one hour address in which you follow up on your 1974 National Union of Christian Schools (NUCS) convention address and speak about leadership responsibility as it applies to school principals in relation to pedagogy, staff, students, and community.

I do not know if I can or will satisfactorily touch on all these aspects in exactly this way. But, I do propose to fulfill my assignment by reviewing my NUCS address, and by calling your attention to leadership responsibilities as they relate specifically to your task as the principals of Christian schools.

**Review of the 1974 NUCS Convention Address, "Leadership and the Christian Community"**

In the NUCS address, I began by pointing out that God has purposed to accomplish His will in this world through the *community* of His redeemed people. The Bible tells us that in the beginning God created the heavens and the earth and human beings in His image. These human beings were given the task of ruling, exercising dominion over the creation (Genesis 1:28); and they were to do this, not in isolation from

---

Speech delivered at the Ontario Christian Schools Principals' Conference, Brampton, Ontario, May 2, 1975.

one another, but as members of a covenantal community and according to the will of their covenant God.

Sometime after the beginning, according to Genesis 3, the first human beings, Adam and Eve, fell into sin. When they fell the whole human race fell and, along with the entire creation, was estranged from God. The human community continued to work in the creation, but did so according to its own desires and in opposition to the will of God.

In the fullness of time (Galatians 4:4) God sent His Son, the last Adam, to His sin-cursed world to take over where the first Adam had so miserably failed. The nature of His work was essentially redemptive. God's Son, Jesus Christ, was born into a world under the curse of sin and it was His task to redeem God's elect sons and daughters from that curse and to restore the entire creation to His Father. By means of His death and resurrection Christ performed His redemptive work. Ascending into heaven, He was made to sit at His Father's right hand from which, through His Word and Spirit, He rules the entire creation kingdom. From the time of His ascension and until His return on the clouds of heaven, it is His ongoing purpose to bring to expression the sovereign glory of His Father, through the service of the redeemed community of which He is the Head, in the creation over which He rules as King.

Thus it is that Paul emphasizes throughout his epistles that the redeemed are made one body in Christ in order that they may walk worthy of the calling they have received (Ephesians 4).

Further, I tried to make clear that the redeemed, Christian community cannot function effectively without *leadership*—leadership that God provides through the appointment of people to particular offices. Indeed, it is Christ who has been appointed by God the Father to be Lord and King over all things. But Christ exercises His office before God through the agency of the new humanity, the community of the redeemed.

As for how that community is able to fulfill its responsibility, its task, its duty before God in this world, I pointed out that it is Christ who enables the redeemed to fulfill their responsibility. First, through His Spirit, Christ causes the redeemed—all the redeemed—to share in His anointing. He places the redeemed—all the redeemed—in office, appointing and qualifying them to administer every part of the creation-kingdom in His Name. Second, by His Word and Spirit, Christ gives direction to the redeemed through the appointment and qualification of leaders.

While it is true that all members of the redeemed community are in office, it must be understood that there is a difference or variety of offices, tasks, and responsibilities in that community. This difference is the result of the different gifts that God gives to the redeemed. Along with each God-given gift comes the responsibility to use that gift in His service. The result is a particular office such as that of teacher, preacher, physician, industrialist, farmer, governor, etc.

These particular offices, brought into being by the gifts of God, coincide with the various social spheres of life. The particular offices do not function without distinction in all areas. Each office has an area, a sphere peculiar to itself. The teacher functions in the area of the school, the preacher in the church, the physician in medicine, the industrialist in production, the farmer in agriculture, the governor in the state, etc. And these people, endowed with special gifts and placed in particular offices, are called *leaders*. They are people—men and women—who have been appointed to and qualified for office. They have been placed at the head of the Christian community in a specific area that, by its very nature, requires the exercise of gifts and offices peculiar to itself. In these positions they are to lead, to direct the redeemed community so that it may fulfill its responsibility before the Lord.

So, you ask, "How does the Christian community fulfill its responsibilities in this world?" The answer is that the Lord qualifies that community by His Spirit and directs that community through leaders endowed with particular gifts who function, of course, according to God's Word.

Finally, in the NUCS address, I attempted to describe the kind of leaders needed by the Christian community and the place of the Christian school in the training and *education* of such leaders. I'm sure that all of us here recognize the responsibility of the Christian school—on all levels—to prepare all members of the Christian community to perform their tasks in God's creation-kingdom. This is the very reason for the establishment of our Christian schools. They exist so that young citizens of the kingdom may come to understand the various areas of the creation and may see that, in each and all of these areas, the Christian community must be prepared to serve Christ as King.

But, it is also the responsibility of the Christian school—especially and increasingly at the higher levels of education—to detect the special gifts given to particular students and to train and prepare them for leadership in the areas corresponding to their gifts. The Christian community needs *qualified* leaders, and much of the responsibility for training that leadership falls on the Christian school. We must assist young people in discovering the gifts that God has given them, encourage them to seek further training relative to those special gifts, and demand that they receive the best training and education for that purpose. I'm not thinking merely of quality education, as that is often understood. Rather, I'm thinking primarily of that kind of education that will enable the occupants of our pulpits to proclaim the whole counsel of God, educators to set forth and apply biblical principles for learning, politicians to articulate a direction for government that will promote justice for all, labor leaders to raise a God-glorifying banner for workmen to follow, and communication experts to establish radio stations and TV centers setting forth a God-centered culture. In other words, I'm thinking of education that is of high quality and in harmony with the Word of God, serving to advance His kingdom.

The Christian community also needs *servant* leaders, i.e., leaders who will function as ruling servants. The Christian leader is a ruler; but he is to rule as a servant, as a servant of God and His people. Therefore, we must make clear, especially to our gifted youth, that they are under authority and that they are being trained to be ministers, servants of the Word of God. In other words: ". . . whoever wants to become great among you must be your servant, and whoever wants to be first must be your slave" (Matthew 20:27). This is our challenge, opportunity, and responsibility—the education and training of qualified leaders who are ready and willing to serve God and His people in bringing to expression the kingdom of Jesus Christ.

And it is within the context of that challenge, opportunity, and responsibility that we now consider:

### The Leadership Responsibility of the Christian School Administrator

It is clear that it is the responsibility of the Christian school to train leaders, prepared to give direction to citizens of the kingdom of Jesus Christ. I wish to make clear further that the Christian school administrator, the principal, occupies a key position within the Christian community that makes him or her a leader in the training of leaders. In doing so, I want to acknowledge that much of my thinking about leadership in the Christian school has been formed by discussions in the Purposes Committee of Dordt College, especially when dealing with matters relating to structure and authority. (The results of this discussion appear in *The Educational Task of Dordt College*, 1979.)

Consider with me, first, the *structure* of a typical Christian educational community. That community, composed of those who recognize the need for biblically-oriented learning, comes to visible expression in the Christian school society. The society—composed not only of parents but also of other members of the covenantal community—is organized to elect a board and to support it, also financially, as it seeks to establish and maintain a Christian school. The board, made up of trusted society members, must set and articulate the basic religious direction of the school, see to the provision of the necessary facilities for carrying on the program of the school, select and make provision for those qualified for teaching and administering the affairs of the school. The teaching staff is called through study and teaching to carry out the central task of the school, that is, to prepare students for the performance of their kingdom responsibilities by leading them into a deeper understanding of the creation. The students are enrolled in the school in order that they may study and learn about the creation-kingdom and their place in it. All of the students are to be trained for kingdom service, and those with special gifts are to be prepared for leadership in areas of the kingdom that call for their particular gifts. Finally, there is the support and maintenance staff, which includes the principal or administrator, appointed to develop and maintain a context in which the work of the school can grow and thrive.

But now, principals/administrators, while you are part of the support staff, you also occupy a distinct position within the larger educational community structure. We have already observed that leaders in the Christian community are to function as *servant* leaders, as servants of God and His people. Before we proceed further, I would like to take a moment to develop this servant concept of leadership.

We must begin with the biblical teaching concerning the sovereignty of God. In His sovereignty God created all things, including human beings. In His sovereignty He commanded them to rule over all things as His servants. Humanity's office and calling was to be a servant of God. By failing to serve God, humanity brought the curse of sin on itself and the entire creation; but God, through Jesus Christ, re-established and republished His sovereignty over all. And in His sovereignty He recreated and redeemed all things, including humanity, and commanded the redeemed to rule over all things as His servants. Redeemed humanity's office, its calling, is to be a servant of Jesus Christ.

In Romans 12:3-8, we read:

> For by the grace given to me I say to every one of you: Do not think of yourself more highly than you ought, but rather think of yourself with sober judgment, in accordance with the measure of faith God has given you. Just as each of us has one body with many members, and these members do not all have the same function, so in Christ we who are many form one body, and each member belongs to all the others.

We have differing gifts, according to the grace given us. If a man's gift is prophesying, let him use it in proportion to his faith. If it is serving, let him serve; if it is teaching, let him teach; if it is encouraging, let him encourage; if it is contributing to the needs of others, let him give generously; if it is leadership, let him govern diligently; if it is showing mercy, let him do it cheerfully.

Please note the following:

"Do not think of yourself more highly than you ought" (12:3). Leadership is not to be used for self-elevation or self-promotion.

"We have differing gifts, according to the grace given us" (12:6). Our talents come from God, and it is in terms of these talents that our offices, our callings, are to be defined.

". . . so in Christ we who are many form one body, and each member belongs to all the others" (12:5). All the redeemed are in office as servants of Christ; each must exercise his or her office for the sake of and in support of others, not for the sake of others but for the sake of Christ.

Did you hear? "Servants of Christ." "For the sake of Christ."

It's important to emphasize that leaders are servants of Christ, especially when we are dealing with leadership in the academic, educational community. Why? Because if formal education is viewed as the task of the church, the leader will be regarded as a servant of the church, directed by church pronouncements and confessions. If education is viewed as the calling of the home, the leader will be seen as servant of parents and subject to their wishes. And if formal education is regarded as the responsibility of the state, the leader will be viewed as a political servant that occupies a position defined by political factors. But we cannot accept any of these options. We recognize that the school must work in close association with the church, family, and state. However, viewing education as servant of any of these institutions fails to acknowledge the kingship of Christ over education. It also fails to recognize the peculiar assignment given to education and the freedom under Christ that education must have if that assignment is to be fulfilled.

The only perspective that consistently recognizes leaders, including educational leaders, as servants of Christ and that helps us to identify the individuals and sub-communities to be served for the sake of Christ, is that of *sphere sovereignty*. When discussing "sovereignty in the sphere of Society" in 1898, Abraham Kuyper notes:

. . . a special higher authority is of necessity involved and this highest authority we intentionally call – *sovereignty in the individual and social spheres*, in order that it may be sharply and decidedly expressed that these different developments of social life have *nothing above themselves but God*, and that the State cannot intrude here, and has nothing to command in their domain. (1931, p. 91)

In a more recent publication, H. Henry Meeter, referring to specific spheres including the school, writes:

> A very important safeguard of popular rights and liberties is to be found in the Calvinistic theory of the sovereignty of each distinct social body in its own sphere, as for example, the home, the school, the church, and commercial and other social organizations. Because each of these organizations is rooted in a principle of its own, has received its own God-given task, and does not owe its rise or existence to the state, the Calvinist maintains that each of these organizations is sovereign whenever it is engaged in matters which relate to its own sphere. (1939, p. 95)

In light of the above, it should be clear that, as servants of Christ in education, it is your calling to assist each of the *sub-communities* in the school—society, board, faculty, student body, support staff—in the performance of their tasks, their callings. And all of this, as we have already indicated, is in order that young citizens of the kingdom may come to understand God's creation, God's world, and their responsibility to serve Him in it.

First, you must assist the **society**. This sub-community is composed not only of parents, but also of grandparents and singles, as well as those who have graduated from the school. Again, once the school has been established, it is the task of the society to elect the board and provide ongoing support for the school. They can provide this support by enrolling their children in the school and also by their gifts and prayers. In order to assist the society in this, you must stay close to them, lead them to a deeper understanding of the meaning and importance of Christian education, keep them informed as to what is going on in the school, and be open to their comments—both positive and negative. Much of this can be accomplished through personal contact, newsletters, articles, meetings, speeches, question-and-answer sessions, etc.

This is a good place to note that, in relationship to the society, we are not describing a calling that is yours alone. Relative to the educational task of the Christian community, the churches also have a supportive duty to perform. By proclaiming the gospel of the kingdom they can make clear the responsibility of their members to serve Christ in all areas, including the area of education. And, by means of church offerings, they can provide financial assistance to parents who find it difficult to meet the costs of Christian education. I am confident that you all know how important this support and assistance can be.

Second, you must be of help to the **board**. It is the task of the board to articulate the religious, confessional direction of the school, to see to the provision of the needed finances and facilities, and to select and secure the services of qualified, dedicated teachers. Obviously, if the board is to perform such an important task, you must assist them in seeing to it that its members are qualified; that they understand the confessional basis of Christian education, how that basis must come to expression in the program of the school, and what is then demanded in terms of facilities, faculty, curriculum development, administration, etc. Only then can you expect the board to give good direction, provide adequate facilities, hire and adequately pay qualified teachers, and support you in the administration of the academic program.

Third, you must support the faculty, the **teaching staff**. This is, obviously, a special area of concern and responsibility. It is the duty of the teachers to prepare students academically for the performance of their kingdom responsibilities by leading them to a deeper understanding of creation and its history, as well as to their place in the creation-kingdom. And it is your responsibility as chair of the faculty— which I assume most of you are—to assist the teachers by giving them direction in the development of the curriculum, in the refinement of pedagogy, in understanding and using the most appropriate educational concepts, and in appreciating what it means to be a Christian educator.

To accomplish this, you must lead teachers to be a community of kingdom workers. This will involve seeing to it that they share an integral Christian perspective on their task. Fundamental differences at this point can tear a teaching staff apart. Further, you must give the teachers direction each day as they pray, discuss, work, and struggle together in bringing this perspective to expression in the development of curriculum, course content, pedagogy, etc. I am becoming increasingly convinced that one of the basic ingredients in Christian education must be a faculty united before one God, according to one Word, seeking to understand an organically united creation as it develops an integrated curriculum that will prepare covenant youth at all levels for service in the one kingdom of our Lord Jesus Christ.

Permit me to give you just one example of why it is important for faculty to work together in community. Some time ago it was my privilege to lead a Teachers' Institute sectional dealing with the matter of sex education in our Christian schools. In reporting on our discussion in

*Christian Educators Journal,* I noted the following:

> We asked ourselves this question: how, by means of the curriculum, can we attain the goals which have been established? We began with certain presuppositions. In the Christian school we are busy studying God's creation in the light of the Scriptures. God's creation, including the structure of man's societal relationships, must be reflected in the curriculum. In this sense creation sets or determines the curriculum.
>
> Within the context of these presuppositions, we sense that it is a mistake simply to present a course in sex education. The danger in doing this, and nothing more, is that sex will be viewed in abstraction from the rest of man's existence and the creation order. We concluded that because sex is but one part of man's existence, and because sex must be seen in relationship to the rest of his existence and the entirety of the created order, it is proper and desirable to offer a course in sex education but, at the same time, it is necessary to deal with sex as it appears in other courses. . . . In this way either ignoring or making too much of sex can be avoided. (Hulst, March 1974, p. 19)

But, don't you see, it is impossible to deal with sex education in this way without working together, communally as a faculty, taking into consideration the entire school curriculum? And, don't you see that this communal approach will not occur without your constant, sensitive leadership?

Fourth, and finally, providing servant leadership for the society, board, and faculty, you will be able to minister to the needs of your **students**. You do, of course, have a responsibility to the children and young people in your school. They must be led to know and understand the various aspects of God's creation in light of God's Word and to see that in all areas they must be prepared to serve Christ their King. In the process, they must discover the talents God has given them and, at the same time, develop their talents so they may not only serve but provide leadership in the kingdom. However—and this brings all aspects of your leadership together—you can fulfill your responsibility to the students only by creating and maintaining a context in which the educational work of the school can grow and thrive. This, of course, will involve leading the society in support of the school, leading the board in setting the direction of the school, and leading the teachers in bringing the students to a greater understanding of creation and its history.

## Conclusion

In conclusion, I would like to speak a word about your relationship to one another as academic leaders. It was not long ago that I received a letter from the frustrated principal of a small Christian school. He wanted, as he should, to bring into the teaching staff of his school qualified teachers with a kingdom perspective; but he was frustrated in doing so because these teachers were being snatched away by larger schools in larger metropolitan areas. As a result, he wrote this letter:

> I never saw such individualism as I have seen in the past month. I don't know if there is a way to work together. The principals here are in a panic, and I know the college kids are too. To me it doesn't seem to be the communal Christian way of looking at things, but then I'm beginning to think that that is a farce. When I first came I wrote letters to some of the principals about different things I needed help with and I was told they appreciated the fact that I wanted to develop our school curriculum etc., but they didn't have the time to help—and those were schools with a good perspective.
>
> I guess I'm wondering what is leadership and how do we express it?
>
> At times I was very disillusioned, but I guess I can't get top notch stuff here, but I don't know if that's right either. Several other principals in the small schools feel the same way. They feel trapped, stuck! It's a vicious circle really, because if you don't have good teachers you don't have good teaching, if you don't have good teaching you don't attract people, and if you don't have people you can't get the vision out.

I don't understand every sentence in this letter, but the main point is obvious. Difficult though it may be, you must work together as Christian school principals, servant leaders in promoting the total program of Christian education. I know this takes people with a large vision, but that is what God and His people expect of those who lead in the education of kingdom servants and kingdom leaders.

**References**

Dordt College. (1979). *The educational task of Dordt College.* By the Dordt College Faculty, Sioux Center, Iowa.

Hulst, J. (March 1974). *Christian Educators Journal,* 16:1.

Meeter, H. H. (1939). *The basic ideas of Calvinism.* Grand Rapids, MI: Baker.

Kuyper, A. (1931). *Calvinism: six Stone Foundation lectures.* Grand Rapids, MI: Eerdmans

# Chapter Six

**To the Reader —**

When this "Creating a Community" speech was delivered, I was travelling in Australia, speaking at a number of Christian School conferences. I was scheduled to spend time with school principals to address the issue of the Christian School community and its ability to provide an environment for Teacher Appraisal and Development. It was a fruitful discussion in that it produced an awareness of the importance not only of teacher appraisal and development, but also of the significance of this taking place in the context of the Christian School community.

Knowing that the Christian School Teachers Conference was also meeting at that time, I was asked if I would be willing—building on the discussion with the principals—to speak to the teachers specifically about community. I hesitated because I had not prepared for this. But, believing that it was important for the teachers to know that the principals had been talking about their appraisal and development in the context of community, I agreed to this request.

Given the fact that I did not have much time to prepare, the reader may notice that, while there are a few biblical references, there are no endnotes. Nonetheless the presentation reflects the result of research done in preparation for discussions with the principals and with others in the broader Christian educational community.

# Creating a Community

It is good to be with you. I enjoyed the time spent with the school principals in Melbourne, and I look forward to this time with you as well.

While meeting with your schools' principals, I was asked to address the issue of the Christian school community—specifically its importance as an environment for Teacher Appraisal and Development. I was very encouraged by my discussions with your principals. They are keenly aware that effective teacher appraisal and development require a communal context and perspective, as well as a supportive communal effort. They encouraged me to address the matter of creating a Christian school community. The two topics are closely related, and yet distinct. Today the question is: How do we create the community that is so important for teacher appraisal and development?

## Creating a Community

I often perceive a sense of loneliness, individually, among Christian school teachers. Most of you work alone in your classroom with your students. After hours you sit alone evaluating the work and progress of your students, preparing lessons and tests for tomorrow's classes. As a result, you may feel distant from others, including fellow teachers. In addition, I know that many of you struggle with feelings of isolation, e.g., isolation from what often appear to be judgmental board members, demanding administrators, competitive faculty members, overly protective parents, and unappreciative students.

However, you need not and should not feel lonely or isolated— because you are not alone. As this conference's theme suggests, as Christian school teachers you are members of a community, a community of which Christ in the Head.

## Community Established

Our theme may give the impression that it is up to us to create a community by and for ourselves. Such is not the case. In fact, if left to

---

Presentation to the Conference of Christian School Teachers, Perth, Australia, March 1991.

ourselves we are inclined to separation, conflict, and disunity. The community of which we are members is created by God through Jesus Christ. He may use us to bring the community to expression. He may use us also to develop, strengthen, expand, and enhance the community. But ultimately the community to which we belong is the creation of God, through Christ, by the Spirit.

This, as perhaps you already know, is how it happened. In the beginning, God brought into being His creation-kingdom, creating man and woman in His image to serve as His representatives, not merely as individuals but together as a human community. Because of the fall into sin the human community experienced conflict, conflict with God and within the community itself. Sin tears apart, sin hurts, sin hinders and is harmful to the community. In the fullness of time (Galatians 4:4), God through Christ redeemed the creation and those elected to represent Him, restoring them to fellowship with Himself and with one another. The redeemed are made members of the Body of which Christ is the Head that they may serve Him, not as individuals but as a community, as members of one another. In the last day, Christ will return to bring His redemptive work to completion that we may live in perfect community with Him in the new heavens and earth (Isaiah 65:17).

The point? When we talk about "Creating a Community," we're talking about bringing to expression what God has created. We're talking about what God has already brought into being.

**Community Developed**

Originally the human community came to expression in a single unit, i.e., the family. It was in the context of this single unit that God made covenant with humanity, a covenant that included a call to serve and a promise to bless. It was in the community of the family that food was produced, children were educated, authority was exercised, and God was worshipped.

Again, initially the human community was one, simple, single family unit. But, as the family went about the performance of its tasks, the human community became more complex; differentiation occurred; and identifiable task communities emerged in which God was to be served. The family, of course, continued with its primary task of nurturing children. But, in addition, under the providential guidance of God, there emerged in the course of time the task communities of worship, called the church; authority or government, called the state; education, called the school; etc.

To this very day, each covenantal task community functions *coram deo*, before the face of God. Each community receives its assignment from God and is responsible to God in the performance of that assignment. You are members of the task community called "school." Your assignment from God is that of education. Other communities, such as the home, the church, and the state, are also involved in education; but education, formal education is the task primarily of the school. Further, as you are well aware, you are called to carry out your assignment in a Christian school, its academic program centered in Christ and based upon His Word, in light of which you are to view each subject as you prepare your students for life and service in the kingdom.

**Community Described**

In the training and education of children, the school works in close association with other task communities, not only but also and especially with the home and the church.

As I have already indicated, while the school attends to formal education, the home is responsible for lovingly nurturing children in the fear of the Lord, and the church, through preaching and teaching, is called to minister to the faith life of children, leading them to a biblically informed public confession of their faith in Christ as Savior and Lord. Obviously, the school should and will want to support both the home and church in carrying out their responsibilities; and, at the same time, the school should be able to count on the support and encouragement of the home and church.

So, you see? You are not alone. The Christian school is part of a community, a supportive community. Therefore, there should be no indifference or harmful competition among you. Instead, there should be ongoing conversation reflecting a concern to understand, encourage, and support one another as home, church, and school work together in the performance of their respective God-given tasks relative to the training of our covenant youth.

But, just as there is a supportive community *around* the school, so there is a community *within* the school. As within other task communities, so also within the school, there are what we call special offices to which people are assigned for the performance of specific tasks. There is the office of the governing board member, with the primary task of giving confessional direction to the school; the office of administrator and staff, with the task of creating and maintaining a context that is conducive to learning; the office of teacher, with the task of providing instruction; and the office of student, with the task of learning—under the leadership of the teacher.

Obviously, if the task of the school is to be accomplished, those occupying the various offices must not work in opposition or at cross purposes but must work together in cooperation and in support of one another. The governing board must set a good, biblical direction. The administration must develop a context that is friendly to a biblical direction. The teachers must provide instruction that reflects a biblical direction. The students must follow the direction of the teachers. As a result, by working together—board, administration, teachers, students—the purpose of the school may be realized.

You see? You are not alone. You are part of a community, a supportive community.

Further, just as there is a community around the school and within the school, so there is a community that *is* the school, which is at the heart of school. We're speaking, of course, of the faculty, the teaching staff.

This community, the faculty, can also be differentiated. The members of the faculty have different gifts and interests: they are trained in different disciplines, and they teach at different levels. Still, they need one another. It would seem that the one who teaches grade four needs to be in conversation at least with those who teach grades three and five—building on grade three and preparing for grade five. The one who teaches reading must work in close association with the one who teaches language. And the one whose strength is in pedagogy should stay close to and work with the one who is gifted with philosophical insight.

You understand, don't you? If and when this happens, you are not alone. You are part of a community, a supportive community.

But this doesn't always happen, does it? It doesn't always happen that the church, home, and school support one another. The home may quibble with the school over the cost of tuition. The church may fail to emphasize the importance of the school in preparing covenant children for the kingdom life. Or the school may see itself in competition with the mission of the church. In any case, when a sense of cooperation is missing, every task community suffers—the home, church, and school.

It doesn't always happen that the board, administration, faculty, and students function cooperatively. It strikes me that when the North Central Accrediting Association conducts its regular 10-year site visit at a school such as Dordt College, it insists upon interviewing not only those directly responsible for the academic program, but also others from the board, administration, staff, faculty, and student body. The Association hopes that the responses to their inquiries will indicate a unity of commitment to the program and purposes of the College, realizing that conflict within and between these groups will inevitably hinder the school in responding to its calling, especially as a Christian academic institution.

Nor does it always happen that faculty members or departments acknowledge their need for one another. Instead, competition and conflict often bring division where a spirit of cooperation and community is essential. Over the years I have spent in Christian higher education I have witnessed firsthand the harmful results of institutional failure on this score. I have in mind a situation in which there were not only differences of opinion on or approach to certain issues, but these differences led to charges of heresy by one group over-against another. What was most troublesome was the fact that students were drawn into the conflict, with the result that their education was being hindered. In the end, the board decided to release the most adamant faculty members, not because of differences of opinion, but because of judgmental attitudes toward colleagues—attitudes that made an effective communal working relationship impossible.

No, it doesn't always happen that we work together as members of a supportive Christian academic community. As a result, as I mentioned earlier, many of us are lonely, many of us are not enjoying our work, and many of us are not as effective as we might or should be. This last item should cause all of us great concern. As a community, we're involved in the work of educating youth of the covenant for life as citizens of the kingdom of Jesus Christ. Conflict and division in that community hinders us in that work and is harmful to our students—which displeases our Lord. Actually, according to Ephesians 2:2, such conflict pleases Satan who, working in constant opposition to Christ and His kingdom, is ever-present "in those who are disobedient."

All of this should awaken us to the fact that creating a community requires:

## Community Effort

No doubt, you have often heard it said concerning marriage that good marriages don't just happen: they call for time, effort, and hard work. So it is with creating and developing a community. The community is actually present, i.e., it has been created by God through Christ and the Spirit of Christ. But, bringing that community to expression requires time, work, and effort on the part of all of the members of that community.

I haven't come to you with a magic formula for developing such a community here in Perth, Australia. That development calls for your time, your work, and your effort. But I can give you an example of that spirit operative in a Christian school community.

Some time ago, I was invited to spend a day at a Christian high school in Edmonton, Alberta. At the beginning of the day, I had breakfast with a group of pastors. We spent time in prayer for Christian education on all levels, and then went on to talk about the importance of the church in promoting Christian schooling. During the rest of the morning, I spoke with the 12$^{th}$ grade, graduating class about continuing their education at a Christian college. In the afternoon, I spent time with the 11$^{th}$ grade class discussing a biblical concept of community. These two hours were particularly interesting because the class had recently visited a Hutterite colony. After the official school day had ended, I met with the faculty to consider a paper dealing with a Christian perspective for physical education and a sports program. Finally, in the evening I attended a Home and School meeting—parents and teachers—where the topic had to do with the discipline of children.

At the end of that day, I was exhausted but I had witnessed and participated in a beautiful example of how to develop a Christian school community. The day was unusual in its intensity, but it was also impressive in indicating what the development and maintenance of a Christian school community requires. And what does it require?

First, developing and maintaining a Christian school community requires *prayer*. As we have seen, it is God who by His Spirit brings the community into being. Therefore, aware of our dependence upon God, we must continually be in prayer that God by His Word and Spirit will enable us to work together as a supportive community. We cannot do this in and of ourselves. We are dependent on the Word and Spirit of our Lord, who Himself prayed "that they may be one as we are one" (John 17:11). And so we must pray for the school community, i.e., the community within the school—our students, our fellow teachers, the administrative staff, the board, and the society—that we may work together as one in Christ. And we must pray for the communities around the school—especially the family and the church—that we may work in support of one another. We need one another, but all of us are dependent upon God and must pray together for His blessings.

Second, if we are going to develop and maintain a Christian academic community, we must have *contact* with one another. This contact can occur primarily through communication, and this communication can take place in a variety of ways. For example, the school can communicate with the home and church through newsletters; with the board by way of reports; with the administration in regular teachers meetings; with fellow faculty members in work sessions; and, of course, by speaking and listening to students in class. Communication must always be two-way communication, with listening just as important as speaking. I know that all of this sounds very challenging, and it is. But indications are that modern technology, if properly used, promises to make such contact much easier and more effective in days to come.

Third, a working Christian school community needs a shared understanding of *task*. There are various ways to describe the task of a Christian school community. In general it may be said that, by way of its curriculum, the school is to lead students to a biblical understanding of God's creation-kingdom and their calling or place in that kingdom. But within that general description, it must be noted that each person or group of persons must understand their part in this educational task. For example, the home, church, and school must understand their respective tasks relative to the education of covenant youth. Also, the board, administration, faculty, and students must clearly understand their callings as members of the school community. Without such understanding, there is bound to be neglect, overlapping, or conflict with the result that the overall educational program will be hindered or harmed.

Fourth, a shared and accepted *perspective* is required. A number of institutions in North America are presently engaged in discussing the possibility of establishing a Reformed university in North America. (They have been challenged to do so by an international conference of institutions of Christian higher education held some years ago in The Netherlands.) Before considering organization, hiring of faculty, curriculum, etc., they have spent close to two years formulating a Reformed perspective by way of a basis and purpose statement. Those of us involved in this project know of universities that were never established because the sponsoring group could not agree on a purpose statement. We also know of universities that were established but came upon difficult times because they lacked a mutual understanding of or commitment to a statement of purpose. The college with which I am associated has developed a clear, biblical, Reformed statement of purpose. The statement doesn't simply take up space on a shelf. Instead, under the direction of a Purposes Committee, it is continually read, discussed, revised, updated, expanded, and put into practice as the college community seeks to fulfill its academic calling. A healthy Christian educational community needs a clearly stated, understood, and agreed upon Christ-centered perspective.

Finally, and most importantly, developing and maintaining a Christian school community requires *love*, in the words of the Great Commandment, love for God and for one another (Matthew 22:37–40). The biblical concept of love is closely associated with obedience. In John 14, for example, Jesus says, "If you love me, you will obey what I command," (vs. 15) and "If anyone loves me, he will obey my teaching" (23). It's clear, isn't it? To love God is to obey His commands, His teaching. And since His commands and teachings cover the entirety of life, loving God means to obey Him everywhere and in all things. Further, to love one another is to help one another obey the commands and teachings of God everywhere and in all things.

As the president of Dordt College, I have always tried to be a "servant leader." Did I always succeed? No, but I tried and asked for forgiveness when I failed. In light of the Great Commandment, I have felt that as a servant leader it was my responsibility to obey God and to assist others—association, board, staff, faculty, students—in obeying, fulfilling their responsibilities to God. As a result, I could be genuinely thankful when others or the College as a whole were recognized for work well done.

Speaking to you, as members of the Christian academic community, it's clear that the Great Commandment requires that we assist the home and church in fulfilling their God-given responsibilities to covenant youth, and that we together work in support of board members, administrators, students, and fellow teachers. All of us must work together in love, otherwise we will not be able to satisfactorily perform the task that God has given us, i.e., to lead covenant youth to an understanding of their call to kingdom service.

God, through the Spirit of Jesus Christ, has created the community of which we are a part. Maintaining and developing that community requires prayer, contact, an understanding of our task, a commitment to perspective, and love. And the greatest, the most important of these, is love (1 Corinthians 13:13).

# Chapter Seven

**To the Reader –**

In August 1981, I was invited to Nigeria to address the Hillcrest Christian School Teachers Retreat. It was the summer following the completion of my doctoral studies in Religion and Higher Education, and a year prior to my being appointed president of Dordt College. I mention this because those who invited me suggested that I focus on the distinctives of a Reformed approach to Christian education, since those attending the Retreat would represent a variety of perspectives on Christian education. Obviously, I was being given a wonderful opportunity at a significant time in my professional life to give expression to my thoughts about an always important topic to what proved to be a highly receptive audience.

I left for Nigeria shortly after participating in the Third International Conference of Institutions for Christian Higher Education at Dordt College— a gathering of representatives of Christian colleges, universities, and seminaries from throughout the world. Anne Maatman, who was in charge of travel for the international conference, graciously arranged my trip so that I was able to spend three days in London and in Paris on the way to Nigeria, and a similar amount of time in Rome and Amsterdam on the return. I spent time sightseeing in London, Paris, and Rome, but in Amsterdam I was invited by the administration of the Free University of Amsterdam to discuss issues relating to the organization now known as the International Association for the Promotion of Christian Higher Education (IAPCHE). I had many interesting experiences on that trip, but one of the most surprising and delightful was running into a recent Dordt graduate as I was watching the changing of the guard at Buckingham Palace, London.

I spent my first evening in Kano, Nigeria, visiting with a Nigerian pastor who was on his way to the United States for a graduate program in theology. During our conversation I asked him what he saw as the greatest need of the Christian community in Nigeria. His immediate response was, "We need a Christian college." This was one of many conversations leading some years later to the establishment of a Christian college in Mkar, Nigeria.

The first planned event of my visit to Nigeria was the Hillcrest Christian School Teachers Retreat held in Jos. After this retreat, I travelled by mission plane to various mission stations. I had many unforgettable experiences on that tour. I saw polio survivors pulling themselves along on the ground with blocks of wood in their hands—a sight that touched me because both my wife and I are polio survivors. As a pastor, I was asked to pray with a widow who was in her small room surrounded by weeping women, while the men stood outside near the open grave of the widow's husband who was soon to be buried. When we were ready to leave, the pilot was asked if we had room in the plane for a woman who had delivered one twin and was unable to deliver the other. We flew her to a nearby hospital, but never heard whether the mother and second baby survived this ordeal.

Just before leaving Nigeria, I was asked to stop at the mission hospital because someone there wanted to see me. When I entered the hospital room I was amazed to see a nurse from McNally, Iowa, a small settlement just west of Ireton, the location of the first congregation I served. The nurse had been attacked by an intruder who broke into her apartment looking for drugs. The only communication available in that area at that time was short-wave radio and regular mail. She not only wanted a pastoral visit, but she asked me to inform her family when I returned to the United States that she was recuperating well.

Back to the Christian School Teachers Retreat—the theme chosen for the Retreat was "A View from the Christian Classroom." I was asked to prepare for six sessions, which I did under the following titles:

1. A View of the World
2. A View of Christ
3. A View of the Bible
4. A View of the Child
5. A View of the Christian Life
6. A View of the Teacher

What follows is a condensed version of these six presentations.

# A View from the Christian School Classroom

As Christian school teachers I am confident that you share with me the conviction that Christian education—if it is to be truly Christian—must in every part be different, distinctive. In other words, the Christian school classroom must at least have a distinctively biblical view of the world, Christ, the Bible, the child, the Christian life, and the teacher. If it doesn't, it will not be truly Christian or worth the effort, time, and money that truly Christian education requires.

First, the Christian school classroom must have a biblical view of the **world**, the cosmos.

I begin with the world because it is the purpose of education to lead children to an understanding of the world and its history. God's world needs to be reflected in the school curriculum, and it is for life in the world that we seek to prepare those whom we educate.

Taking our stance in the Bible, we see the world as God's creation. God created all things in heaven and on earth (Genesis 1:1), including "man in his own image" (Genesis 1:27). Everything we consider in our classrooms is the creation of God. The Bible also tells us that God created by His Word (Genesis 1:3) and by His Spirit (Genesis 1:2), which shows that the world cannot exist or be understood apart from God and His Word.

The world belongs to God and is subject to God and His Word (Psalm 119:89–91). The world is, therefore, the kingdom of God. As S. G. De Graaf writes, referring to Genesis 1: "The institution of the Kingdom of God is central to this chapter" (De Graaf, 1977, p. 29). The world, the kingdom of God exists for a purpose, namely, the glory of God (Romans 11:36). This purpose can be attained only by submission to the Word of God. In the beginning everything God created was capable of fulfilling that purpose, which is why "God saw all that he had made, and it was very good" (Genesis 1:31).

God realizes the purpose of His creation kingdom through "male

---

Hillcrest Christian School Teachers Retreat, Jos, Nigeria, August 1981.

and female," the crown of His creation (Genesis 1:27–31). As image-bearers of God, they are mandated to exercise dominion over the creation-kingdom, discover its laws, work within creation according to these laws, and bring the fruit of their work in praise to God. But, through their fall into sin, they rejected this mandate (Genesis 3). Instead of regarding the creation as God's kingdom, they make it an object of exploitation for their own satisfaction and glory (Genesis 3:6). Through the redemptive work of Jesus Christ, graciously promised in the Garden (Genesis 3:15) and realized in the fullness of time (Galatians 4:4), God reclaims the creation as His kingdom and summons the redeemed to work for the expression of His kingdom everywhere (Matthew 28:19–20).

The Christian classroom views the world as the creation-kingdom of God. The redeemed are mandated "to work it and take care of it" (Genesis 2:15). But since this involves discovering and gaining insight into creation's laws, education is essential in the performance of this mandate. Acquiring this insight involves scholarship—studying, examining, understanding the creation. Further, the results of this study must be transmitted from one generation to the next. This involves covenantal education, Christian education—enabling children to understand the world, God's creation-kingdom, in light of His Word.

Second, it should be clear from the above that the Christian school classroom requires a biblical view of the **Christ**.

We could at this point declare our belief in Jesus Christ as the eternal Son of God; incarnate in human flesh; possessing a human and divine nature in one divine person; bearing names such as Jesus, Christ, Lord, Son of God, Son of Man; crucified, risen, ascended, present with and in us by His Spirit, and coming again to judge the living and the dead. And we certainly want to affirm that we confess and believe all this. But more must be said if we would gain a fully biblical view of Christ and understand the significance of this view specifically for the work of Christian education.

To do so, we must see Christ as the agent of *creation*, the One through whom God brings His creation-kingdom into being. John declares in the prologue of his gospel that the Word by which all things were created in the beginning was Christ (John 1:1–3). The writer of Hebrews states that He who is the effulgence of God's glory, the very image of His substance, appointed heir of all things—Jesus Christ—is the same one by whom He made the universe (Hebrews 1:1–3). In other words creation is brought into existence and is sustained by Christ. Therefore, creation and its history, which education seeks to understand, cannot be understood apart from Christ.

Further, we must see Christ as the agent of *recreation*. Earlier we noted that Christ, by His death and resurrection, reclaimed creation as the kingdom of God and the redeemed as citizens of the kingdom, i.e., those who would serve Him in His kingdom. This is clearly revealed in the Old Testament. God formally established His covenant with Abraham, promising that through Abraham and his seed (out of whom would come the Christ) all the nations of the earth would be blessed (Genesis 12). God promised to David that his kingdom would endure forever (2 Samuel 7) and that One would come to sit on his throne who would make his kingdom a universal kingdom (Psalm 2:8–9). That One was Christ.

This truth is also revealed in the New Testament. When Christ was introduced, John the Baptist called the people to repentance because the King and the kingdom were at hand (Matthew 3). By His death and resurrection, Christ overcame the kingdom enemies of sin, Satan, and death; reclaimed the creation as the kingdom arena in which God was to be served; and purchased with His blood those who were and are to serve as citizens of the kingdom (Colossians 1, Ephesians 1). When Christ ascended into heaven, He laid hold of the scepter of universal authority (Acts 1:1–11, Matthew 28); He returned in the power of the Spirit to anoint the redeemed for their task (Acts 2), and He now rules all things for the well-being of His people (Ephesians 1:22) unto the glory of the Father (Hebrews 1). Someday, Christ will return to complete the perfection of the kingdom—the new heavens and earth (Revelation 21:1–3)—and the citizens of the kingdom (1 Corinthians 14:42–58). He will then present the perfected kingdom to the Father, that He may be all in all (1 Corinthians 15:28).

I was travelling with a Dordt College recruiter to speak to a group of prospective students at a school in Neerlandia, Alberta—approximately 90 miles north of Edmonton. Since this was our first trip to Neerlandia, we wondered how we would know which school to go to. Suddenly we came upon a building in one window of which was a large sign: CHRIST IS KING! "That's it!" I said. Yes, that is it. The view from the Christian school classroom acknowledges that Christ is King.

Third, we consider how the Christian school classroom views the **Bible,** more precisely how it views the relationship of the Bible to the task of the Christian school.

To do so we must go back to the beginning in which God, as we have already seen, created all things by His Word. God also created man and woman in His image, enabling them to know Him and the creation according to His Word and to know themselves as servants of God's Word in the creation. Subsequently, the man and the woman fell into sin. In spite of the fall, however, they remain God's image-bearers (Genesis 5:1) and the creation remains a cosmos (Colossians 1:17) subject to God's Word. But, because of the fall, they no longer acknowledge God as Creator and Lord; they no longer see the creation as cosmos, functioning according to God's Word and unto His glory; and they no longer know themselves as God's servants in His world (Romans 1). Clearly the results of the fall are tragic, especially for education, because the man and woman no longer correctly understand themselves, the world, or their place in the world.

God, therefore, comes and speaks to the fallen in human language with His Word of redeeming grace (Genesis 3:15). In the fullness of time, that Word became flesh, the Christ (John 1:14). All of this, the history of the redemptive work of God in Christ, is infallibly recorded in the Bible, the inscripturated Word of God (2 Timothy 3:15–17). The Bible, the *inscripturated* Word of God, points to Christ, the *incarnate* Word of God, by means of which the *creational* Word of God can once again be understood.

And this, it seems to me, sets forth the basic relationship of the Bible to education. I understand Christian education to be that activity whereby we endeavor to prepare children to live as God's servants in His world, with the Bible as essential to that endeavor. No, I'm not saying that the Bible is a textbook for science and education. Those who use it as such misuse the Bible. Nevertheless, it is only in light of the Bible that both teacher and student can come to know God as Creator of heaven and earth, themselves as God's representatives in His world, and the cosmos as functioning under God's law, God's Word.

Another way of stating the case is to use the example of John Calvin in referring to the Bible as "spectacles" (Calvin, 1936, p. 80). According to this analogy, we are *spectators*, the creation is the grand *spectacle*, and the Bible is the *spectacles* through which we view and come to understand the creation and our place in it.

Fourth, it is essential that we consider how the **child** is to be viewed in the Christian school classroom. This view will, of course, seek to understand the child in relationship to God—created, fallen, and redeemed in Christ.

The view that approaches the matter apart from God typically focuses on only one aspect of the child's being. One such view defines the child merely as a *rational being*. This is the stance of the curriculum-centered approach, which tends to reduce the child to an intellectual absorber of information. Others see the child solely as a *biological organism* that has developed a complex nervous system. This is the evolutionistic approach that views education as a matter of teaching the correct responses to a system of rewards and punishments. Still others view the child as nothing more than a *social being*. This is a horizontal approach, which regards the teacher's responsibility merely as that of developing the child's social functions. The same reduction occurs when the child is viewed primarily as a *moral, economic,* or *spiritual being*. In each instance, the child is reduced to less than what God intended.

A biblical view, instead of concentrating on just one aspect, views the child as God's image-bearer, created a *religious being* that is able from the heart (Proverbs 4:23) to respond to the Word in all aspects of life. In this perspective, the Christian school teacher leads students to see themselves in a restored relationship to God, called to serve Him in His creation-kingdom.

Education out of this perspective requires respect for the child. The child is to be seen not as an animal to be trained or as an object to be manipulated but as a person created in the image of God and capable of responding to God's calling. Further, education from this viewpoint must appeal to the child's sense of responsibility by relating the education received to that calling. Finally, biblically directed education should give guidance in light of the child's religious duty to love God and neighbor (Matthew 22:37–40).

The goal of Christian education is not, first of all, the intelligent, cultured, socially-adjusted, proper, economically successful, or pious person. Since life finds its true meaning in love of God and neighbor, Christian education should always lead to radical discipleship in which the child submits the whole of life to God, is prepared to testify in all things to the newness of life in Christ, and is moved to offer the entirety of life to God as His co-worker.

Fifth, we are led to reflect on how the classroom of the Christian school should view the **Christian life**, the life for which its students are being educated. Briefly stated, the Christian life is an office, a calling received from God. The biblical concept of office refers to how God uses the man and woman to administer the creation. It refers to their stewardship of their lives and of all that has been placed in their care. Paul speaks of himself and the other apostles as "servants of Christ and as those entrusted with the secret things of God" (1 Corinthians 4:1). And Peter states that this stewardship involves every member of the body of Christ:

"Each one should use whatever gift he has received to serve others, faithfully administering God's grace in its various forms" (1 Peter 4:10).

This concept of office finds its origin in the Genesis account of creation. In the beginning, God created all things. The creation belongs to Him (Psalm 24:1–2). But the man and the woman, image-bearers of God, are to have "dominion" over the creation (Psalm 8:3–9), that is, they are to manage, care for the creation as God's representatives, God's stewards. But, as the writer of Hebrews, chapter 2, points out, God's representatives sinned and thus failed in their office as stewards. Therefore God turned to the Christ, the One through whom all things were made (John 1:3).

Christ is put into the office of Servant of God. He is a *suffering servant*—by His suffering and death, He makes peace and reconciles all things on earth and in heaven to the Father (Colossians 1:20). He continues in office as *glorified servant*—ascending into heaven He is given all authority in heaven and on earth so that He may administer the affairs of the restored creation according to the will and unto the glory of God the Father. However, He administers the affairs of the restored creation through the agency of mankind—the unwilling agency of the non-redeemed and the willing agency of the redeemed. Through Christ, the redeemed are restored to office and given the task of administering, "as good stewards," the affairs of creation in the Name of Christ.

As we have seen all the redeemed, as members of Christ's body, are in office. But not all the members of the body are the same. While there is unity in the body that results in the universal office of believers, there is also diversity in the body that results in particular offices. This diversity comes to initial expression in different abilities and qualifications that, in turn, are gifts of God's grace to be used in His service. Thus, some are able to teach, or preach, or rule, etc. (Romans 12:6–8); they are qualified to perform a variety of tasks in the creation-kingdom.

The biblical understanding of office enables each of our students to answer the question, "What am I to do with my life?" Up to this point, we have seen that there is a variety of offices, tasks, responsibilities within the Christian community. This variety is the result of different gifts that God bestows on His people; with each gift comes the responsibility to use that gift in the service of the Lord in the various areas of the creation-kingdom. It is in this connection that the Christian school has an obvious responsibility.

First, the Christian school must prepare its students for the fulfillment of the universal office of the Christian community. This is the very reason for the existence of our Christian schools. They exist in order to bring students to a biblical understanding God's creation, and to make students aware that they are being educated, prepared to serve God in all the various areas of that creation-kingdom. Second, the Christian school must lead each of its students (i.e., those who are in the office of student) to discover, identify, and develop the special gifts God has given them so that, no matter how they answer the question, "What am I to do with my life?" they will be ready to perform their task as servants of Christ according to the will and for the glory of God.

In other words, the students in the Christian school will have a biblical view of the Christian life. They will not suppose that, if they are to serve Christ, they must do so in conjunction with the instituted church—important as the instituted church may be. Nor will they assume that, if they are to lead a Christian life, they must be involved always and everywhere in leading people to salvation—important as it is to lead people to salvation. Rather, they will understand that, no matter what their God-given task or calling may be, they are to be engaged in "works of service" (Ephesians 4:12) in God's creation-kingdom.

Finally, we inquire as to how the **teacher** in the Christian school classroom should be viewed and how we as Christian school teachers should view ourselves.

We conclude with a view of the teacher because the teacher is at the heart of what happens in the Christian school, and because everything we have said up to this point—regarding a biblical view of the world, Christ, child, Bible, and Christian life—is needed to describe and understand how the Christian school should view the teacher. We do not intend to present a long list of an ideal teacher's personal qualities, but rather to speak in terms of the office or calling of the teacher—even as we have spoken in terms of the office and calling of the student.

In this light, it is obvious that the teacher in the Christian school must be a Christian, confessing, "I am not my own, but belong—body and soul, in life and death—to my faithful Savior Jesus Christ" (Heidelberg Catechism, Lord's Day 1, Question and Answer 1). The Christian school teacher must be able personally to acknowledge *Christ* as Savior from sin and as Lord over all of life.

However, more is involved. The Christian teacher must not only be a Christian but must have a Christian perspective on teaching and learning. This means, as we have seen in describing the *Christian life*, that the Christian teacher must have office consciousness, an awareness of being called to be servant of God in all areas of life but particularly in the area of education. Teaching is an office, a task to be performed humbly in dependence upon God, obediently according to the Word of God, and boldly with authority granted by God.

Further, the Christian teacher must have a sense of community. When we think of office and tasks to be performed we must not think just of one person, but of a community of persons. Viewing history from a biblical perspective we see that from various God-given tasks a variety of communities were formed. From the task of propagation and life-enrichment the family was formed (Genesis 4:1, 2); and, from the invitation to worship and call on the Name of the Lord, the instituted church was brought into being (Genesis 4:26b). Throughout human history, we observe the development of distinct task-communities, including the school "to transmit the culture of one generation to the next" (Schrotenboer, 1972, p. 18). In this light, the Christian teacher is not only to be aware of the school's task in distinction from and relationship to other task communities—family, church, work place, state—but also conscious of the importance of working in harmony with, in dependence upon, and in support of fellow Christian teachers.

As a member of the Christian educational community, the Christian teacher must have a biblical view of the *world* as God's creation-kingdom and the responsibility of leading students to understand that world and its history in light of the Word of God, inscripturated in the *Bible*. This, in turn, should move the Christian teacher to seek a biblical understanding of the subject or subjects to be taught. This must be done not only in the case of Bible studies, but also of courses in history, literature, mathematics, geography, biology, art, music—all of them areas within God's grand creation.

Finally, to mention no more, the Christian teacher must have a biblical view of Christian school *students*—respecting and loving them as image-bearers of God, leading them as religious beings to obey the Word of God and viewing them as capable of being able to respond to the biblical guidance given them. In other words, the Christian teacher is a person with a mission. As students are led into an understanding of God's creation-kingdom they are helped, by the teacher, to discover their God-given gifts, to develop those gifts, and to prepare themselves for a specific place, office, task in the kingdom of Jesus Christ.

Therefore, the greatest delight of the Christian teacher—and of the Christian school—is to see students, in the power of the Holy Spirit, qualified to step into office, and committed to seek first the Kingdom of God (Matthew 6:33).

## References

Calvin, J. (1936). *The institutes of the Christian religion.* Philadelphia: Presbyterian Board of Christian Education.

De Graaf, S. G. (1977). *Promise and deliverance.* St. Catherines, ON: Paideia Press.

Schrotenboer, Paul. (1972). *Man in God's world.* Toronto, ON: Wedge Publishing.

# Chapter Eight

**To the Reader –**

When the invitation came from Christian Schools International (CSI) early in 1981 to speak at the Pella Christian Grade School to a workshop on "Teaching Bible in the Christian School," I was very interested. I did not consider myself an expert on the subject, but I was interested, especially because of discussions being held at that time in the Christian school community.

The discussions seemed to be centered around two questions. First, assuming that the training and development of our covenant children takes place primarily in the home, church, and school, what is the relationship of these three social groups to one another as concerns their responsibilities to our children? Second, how do these differing responsibilities reflect themselves in the place of the Bible in each of the three groups, especially in the Christian School? It's true that these two questions are not specifically stated in the paper, but both the questions and the discussions they produced were evident throughout the workshop.

When the workshop was announced, Mr. and Mrs. Glenn Andreas invited me to spend the week as a guest in their home. I greatly appreciated this invitation. Not only did I appreciate the Andreas' hospitality, but also the opportunity to spend time visiting with Glenn Andreas—a close friend of H. Evan Runner and an avid reader of Abraham Kuyper and Herman Dooyeweerd. Since much of my perspective on the assigned topic was shaped by the teachings of Kuyper and Dooyeweerd, and since I had re-read Runner's *The Relation of the Bible to Learning* in preparation for the workshop, I looked forward to sharing my prepared presentations with Glenn and receiving his responses. I was not disappointed. Discussions, long into the evening, proved to be very helpful, as did the conversations with Christian school administrators and teachers during the workshop sessions. The results are reflected in my edited and revised presentation.

Notice that in the introduction I say, "I intend not to talk at you, but with you; not to give answers, but to struggle with you in seeking answers; not to present myself as an expert, but to strive with you for expertise." And that is precisely what happened, which is why I could end the week by saying, "I hope that you and your colleagues will continue to discuss. . . ."

What follows is a summary of five morning presentations. I found it difficult to compress the material into one manageable piece, with the result that parts of the paper are quite compact. But I hope that the end result speaks meaningfully to discussions still taking place around this topic today.

# Teaching Bible in the Christian School

Thank you for inviting me to join you in this workshop on "Teaching Bible in the Christian School." This is an important subject, about which there is some confusion, not only in the Christian schools, but in the Christian community in general.

I have spent some time teaching Biblical Theology at Dordt College, and, in the process, I have gained some experience in teaching Bible in a Christian school setting. Still, in this workshop, I intend not to talk at you, but with you; not to give answers, but to struggle with you in seeking answers; not to present myself as an expert, but to strive with you for expertise. To make progress together in our understanding about teaching Bible in the Christian school, we should first begin by considering:

### The Place of the Christian School in the Christian Community

I wish to define the place of the Christian school in light of the principle of *sphere sovereignty*. I feel a bit defensive in doing so because recent discussions in our community have placed a cloud over this principle. Extremists on one side have promoted the principle to the point of isolating the spheres from one another. Extremists on the other side have reacted by totally rejecting the principle, even though it has for a long time been an essential part of our Calvinist world-and-life-view.

At the conclusion of his lecture at a Unionville Study Conference, H. Evan Runner stated:

> There is no evangelical theme that is more in need of a forceful, relevant interpretation and application to the world of our time than this one of sphere-sovereignty, which you have so patiently listened to me unfold here.... (Runner, 1967, pp. 165–166)

And that is why I am convinced that we cannot rightly understand the place of the Christian school and how to teach Bible in our Christian schools apart from an understanding of and commitment to this principle.

---

A combined summary of five presentations at a Christian Schools International workshop, Pella, Iowa, June 1981.

The principle of sphere sovereignty arises out of a biblical, kingdom view of society. According to this view, God in the beginning brought into being His kingdom and man as His kingdom servant. (I use *man* here and in what follows as meaning "human being," whether male or female.) By the fall into sin, man rebelled against God, choosing instead the lordship of Satan. By His death and resurrection, Christ broke the power of Satan and was made King over all, with the redeemed as His servants. Sphere sovereignty provides us with a view of the kingdom and the spheres within the kingdom. It sees society as composed of a variety of relationships. God alone is sovereign over all of these relationships and has given to each relationship or sphere its own laws, structures, task, and authority for pursuing its kingdom task. As a result, each societal relationship has its own sovereign sphere of authority.

In the beginning, society was undifferentiated, with the various spheres subsumed under the family. But in the course of history, as man performed the work of developing and unfolding the creation, differentiation occurred. Different associations developed according to the creational laws of God, producing

> . . . a wide variety of spheres which arise out of the complex life of mankind, each having its own task to perform, its own mandate entrusted to it by God. Thus there exists the sphere of the family, the sphere of science, of art, of technique and invention, of trade and commerce, of industry, of agriculture, the sphere of the Church. . . . (Meeter, 1939, p. 159)

In each sphere we find a human community working within a particular aspect of the creation. Each sphere has its own type of authority from God and should not presume to have authority over another, e.g., the church over the sphere of the school.

Closely related to sphere sovereignty is the principle of *sphere universality*, i.e., that all of the spheres are intimately connected in unbreakable coherence. Sphere universality teaches not only that the spheres are closely related, but also that each sphere reflects and is reflected in all other spheres. For example the instituted church, which has to do with the faith aspect of life, reflects and is reflected in the spheres of the home, school, and government.

This brings us to consider specifically the sphere of the *school*. According to the principle of sphere sovereignty, the school occupies a distinct sphere with an area of jurisdiction of its own and cannot be reduced to any other aspect of reality. In the beginning education was subsumed under the family; but, as man worked culturally and the functions performed within the family were differentiated, the sphere of education emerged alongside the family and other spheres within society. This does not mean that the school is simply an extension of the home, or that it exists by virtue of parental authority. Focusing on the teacher in the school, H. de Jongste and J. M. van Krimpen observe:

> The parents should not intrude upon that which belongs to the teacher. He has been assigned a task and a duty; he is the responsible person. Responsibility demands conscious freedom of action, a field of action of one's own.... (1968, p. 112)

In other words, no sphere receives authority from another. The school exists by God-delegated authority. It has its own rootage, exists according to its own nature, possesses its own inner principle, and has its own task entrusted to it by God. The school is free from the authority of other spheres in order that it may fulfill its own God-given task and responsibility.

And what is the task of the school? Because of sphere universality, we acknowledge that there is an educational aspect to the task of other spheres. For example, the church teaches the faith, the state gives instruction regarding the laws of the land, and the factory teaches workers how to operate a machine. But the task of the school is that of formal, systematic education. In fulfillment of that task, the school must see to the development of creative scholarship and to the transmission of the knowledge gained so that, by means of formal academic activity, students may become mature citizens of the community and the community may perform its full-orbed task on earth.

The school along with other spheres, such as the home and the church, seek to prepare the child for service in all spheres of the kingdom. At the same time, the school must be distinguished from the home and the church. All three spheres are involved in preparing children for kingdom service, but each does so in a different way. The home is responsible for the total nurture of the child providing first, basic, informal instruction that prepares the child for independent living before the face of God in the whole of life. The church is called through preaching and teaching to give the child confessional training that prepares the child for membership in the church and has as its goal profession of faith. And the school provides the child with academic training by way of teaching in the classroom, introducing the child to all aspects of the creation-order and preparing him/her for kingdom life by analyzing with the child the implications of biblical principles for family, economics, politics, etc.

The *Christian Educators Journal* (April, 1971, pp. 21–24) contains a report to the 1955 Synod of the Christian Reformed Church that makes the same kind of distinctions. The family is seen as foundational in the educational process, giving instruction in the first rudiments of obedient Christian living. The church is charged to give moral and spiritual training, leading the child in faith development, which points to public profession. The school, focusing on the covenant child, is to work for development in all aspects of life by way of an academic program. Thus in Dordt College's statement of purpose, *Scripturally-Oriented Higher Education* we are reminded that

> Education as a distinct sphere in God's kingdom has a specific task to perform. This task can be, and is, rather precisely spelled out. Its task is that of contributing to the development of Christian character through the training of the mind, using various disciplines and skills of learning, and through the transmission of the scholarly knowledge of past generations to the present, together with the necessary evaluation and application, enabling the individual to realize himself as God's image bearer and to fulfill his purpose in human society commensurate with his capabilities and opportunities. (November, 1967, pp. 28–29)

It is important that these distinctions are observed, especially in teaching the Bible. If they are not kept in mind, all kinds of difficulties result. For example, if we fail to distinguish the task of the school from that of the church, we may use the Bible class to evangelize or to catechize—both of which are tasks of the church. Or, if we fail to differentiate between the home and the school—viewing the school simply as an extension of the home—in the end the school will be expected to do what the home is supposed to do but is unable or unwilling to do. On the other hand, some overlapping of tasks notwithstanding, when these distinctions are observed, the home, church, and school should be able to work harmoniously, each doing its appropriate part in teaching the Bible to covenant children.

This understanding of the place of the Christian school in the Christian community provides a context in which to consider:

### The Role of the Bible in the Christian School

Our study suggests that the Bible has primarily three roles in the Christian school.

First, the Bible serves a *perspectival* role. The Bible provides the norms for all of life, but also for educational activity. The Bible is the basis for Christian education. The Christian character of the school depends upon how faithfully the Bible is brought to bear on the total operation of the school, including the activities of the school society, board, administration, support staff, teachers, and students. The educational creed of the school must arise from biblical teaching concerning God, man, and the creation. In light of the concept of sphere sovereignty, this creed should be educational rather than ecclesiastical in nature. As Clarence Bouma noted long ago at a convention of the National Union of Christian Schools:

> The Three Formulas of Unity are not an adequate platform for our Christian School movement. They are ecclesiastical standards and as such I prize them highly, but they are not intended to be and should not be looked upon as an adequate platform for the Christian School movement. . . . Such a distinctive platform is found in . . . that distinctly Christian view of God and the World which has sometimes been indicated by the term "Reformed Principles." (Bouma, 1925, p. 122–123)

In other words, at the heart of the Christian academic enterprise is the development of an educational philosophy where all things, including the subjects taught, are done from a Christian, biblical perspective.

This is not to say that all subjects must be taught from the perspective of biblical studies. This would mean placing biblical study courses above other courses or between the Bible and other disciplines. This we reject because all subjects—including biblical studies—must be approached from the perspective of the Bible. We must teach biology, history, mathematics, and Bible courses from a biblical perspective, because this is what makes a Christian school truly Christian. Indeed, as we hope to show, the Bible has a devotional and educational role in the school; unless the entire program is driven by a biblical perspective, however, the school cannot rightly claim to be Christian. Again, a biblical perspective in every class, every part of its program is what makes a school Christian.

Second, the Bible has a *cultic, devotional, confessional* role in the Christian school. Just as in the family, so it is appropriate and even necessary that the Christian school community gather for daily devotions, chapel, periodic times of worship.

The Bible should be central in these worship gatherings. They should be "Scripturally-oriented devotional . . . activities," (Dordt, 1979, p. 16), centered around the Bible and in response to the Bible. Further, they should be characterized by the nature of the school, which is an academic institution. While church worship focuses on the Christian life in general, school worship should focus on life in and around the school. We should not hear from students, "This is just like church." Rather, it should be evident in both structure and content that this is school worship.

Such devotional activities "ought not to be considered mere additions to the academic task" (Dordt, 1979, p. 16). Rather, they can and should serve to enrich both teachers and students in their commitment to serve the Lord in the school. Hearing the Word and responding by singing, praying, and confessing the faith can be a liturgy for learning. It does not constitute the essence of Christian education or guarantee Christian education in the school. It should not be viewed as a means for integrating faith and learning, but it can point to such integration, which is the task of teachers and students in the classroom. Again, what church worship is to Christian service in all of life, so school worship is to Christian service in every classroom.

Third, the Bible has an *educational, academic* role in the Christian school. The Bible can function as a field of inquiry and an object of study, a subject for careful reflection in biblical studies. Our approach may never belie our confession of and submission to the Bible as divine revelation. Nevertheless, the message of the Bible is anthropomorphic, i.e., it comes to us in various kinds of human literature. There is in the Bible literature such as historical narrative, legal documents, poetry, words of wisdom, parables, and epistles. As such, the Bible is subject to academic use, e.g., analysis of biblical texts, surveys of redemptive history, theoretical reflection on biblical teachings, and academically-oriented student response.

This raises a question: what is the nature and aim of this academic role? Our answer to this question depends in large part upon our anthropology, our view of man and his task in the world. Secular education views man as a "biological organism," subject to various forces and stimuli (DeGraaff, 1978, p. 1). At best, man is a social animal, and his task is to function in a socially acceptable way. In this view, "good teaching is a matter of skillfully manipulating a system of rewards and punishments . . . to condition children to respond in the desired way" (DeGraaff, 1978, p. 2). Christian education rejects the secular position. It views man as an image-bearer of God. Man is a religious being; a responsible, i.e., capable-of-responding being. Man's task, as a religious being, is to respond believingly and obediently to the Word of God in the entirety of life. In this view, "Christian education should always lead to radical discipleship" (DeGraaff, 1978, p. 5).

Many agencies are involved in providing children with guidance in regard to their life's task. Parents provide guidance by way of loving nurture, the church by way of confessional direction, and the school by giving form and shape to the child's analytical functioning. All contribute to the guidance of the child, but the school does so specifically by way of analytical activity, enabling the child to gain an understanding of his/her religious calling in life.

And what is the nature of this analytical activity? Contemporary educational theory faces a dilemma in answering this question. Should the activity be subject-oriented or child-oriented?

The humanistic response tends to be subject-oriented, identifying reality with abstractions and making education a matter of learning facts without getting to the meaning of the facts. On the other hand, modern pragmatism reacts by being child-oriented, concentrating upon the developmental needs of the child to the neglect of the subject matter. Christian education resolves this dilemma by emphasizing the rightful, but limited function of analytical activity (DeGraaff, 1978, p. 12). Analytical activity is not abstract activity, does not reduce reality to scientific concepts, and is not an end in itself. Rightly performed analytical activity is reflection upon real life (What could be more exciting?), is sensitive to the child's developmental limitations and possibilities (What could be more human?), and is designed to help the child understand his/her place and task in the kingdom (What could be more important?).

Biblical studies is but one subject among many, one way to provide the child with a deeper understanding of the Christian, kingdom way of life. However, in order to do this, biblical studies must take its place within the context of the whole of the created order, as that order is reflected in the entire school curriculum. There is a diversity of aspects in the creation—not only the confessional, but also the ethical, political, economic, social, aesthetic, psychic, biotic, numerical, etc. In recognition of this diversity, biblical studies will draw on many disciplines, such as history, geography, and language; biblical studies will also contribute to other disciplines, such as history, literature, sociology, and political theory.

Focusing on the academic role of the Bible in the Christian school, it is also important that we clearly understand:

**The Nature and Authority of the Bible**

The way we use or teach the Bible is going to depend upon how we approach the Bible.

In considering how to approach and interpret the Bible, theologians often distinguish between eisegesis and exegesis. *Eisegesis*, which reads into the biblical text that which is not necessarily in the text, is to be avoided. On the other hand, *Exegesis*, which takes out of the biblical text that which is in the text, is to be encouraged. At the same time, however, this distinction and the warning against reading into the text should not blind us to the fact that all of us approach the Bible from a certain perspective, i.e., we come to the Scriptures with a certain pre-understanding of the Scriptures.

Some insist that we must come to the Bible and, therefore, to the teaching of the Bible without any presuppositions. We must empty ourselves of any and all preconceptions and simply let the Bible speak to us. But, this is impossible. We cannot escape ourselves. We will always be involved in interpreting the Bible. It is not that we must come to the Bible with no perspective; instead, we must come to the Bible with a biblical perspective, i.e., a perspective shaped by the Bible itself.

The importance of a biblical approach to the Bible has become clearer to me as a result of my graduate school experience at the Iliff School of Theology, adjoining the University of Denver. The dominant theology at Iliff is Process Theology—shaped by the philosophy of Alfred North Whitehead and the theology of John B. Cobb Jr. Knowing that this is the dominant theology and perspective of Iliff faculty, one not only knows the approach that will be taken but also the interpretation that will be given and the message that will be derived from the Scriptures. Does this mean that we are caught in a hermeneutical circle? Yes, but the question is not whether or not we are caught in a hermeneutical circle. Rather, the question is shall we work in a biblical or non-biblical hermeneutical circle? Assuming that we are committed to a biblical approach, there are at least two approaches that must be rejected.

First, there is the moralistic approach that reduces the Bible to culturally conditioned categories of good and bad. Each and every part of the Bible becomes a story to which a moral is attached or from which a moral is derived. This approach sees God primarily as a great judge, defines man as a moral being, and views the Bible as a collection of moral axioms. In this view, the purpose of teaching the Bible is not to bring the child to an understanding of his place in the creation, but to build the child's moral character.

Sidney Greidanus calls this the "exemplary approach" to the Bible. This approach:

> . . . sets forth the friendship between David and Jonathan as the ideal friendship to which Christians today must attain . . . .
>
> . . . as the woman reached to touch the border of Jesus' garment, so we must touch the Savior, if only the border of his garment . . . . (1970, pp. 58, 59)

Second, there is the intellectualistic approach that sees God as a knowable object, defines man as a rational being, and views the Bible as a revelation of God's thoughts. In this view, the Bible becomes a "holy source book" for biblical facts, names, dates, places, and events; and the teachings of the Bible are reduced to a number of logical propositions. In this view, the purpose of teaching the Bible is to bring the student to a knowledge of the contents of the Bible, i.e., biblical facts, with little regard for the meaning of these facts for kingdom life.

An example of the kind of thinking that is behind this intellectualism can be found in an article in *The Trinity Review* by Gordon H. Clark titled "God and Logic":

> The well-known prologue to John's Gospel may be paraphrased, "In the beginning was Logic, and Logic was with God, and Logic was God.... In Logic was life and the life was the light of men. (1980, pp. 2, 3)

> Any translation of John 1:1 that obscures this emphasis on mind or reason is a bad translation. And if anyone complains that the idea of *ratio* or debate obscures the personality of the second person of the Trinity, he should alter his concept of personality. In the beginning, then, was Logic.

It is our conviction that, instead of a moralistic or intellectualistic approach, a biblical approach to the Bible requires an historical-redemptive interpretation of the Scripture, which acknowledges the *confessional* character of the Bible. According to this view, the Bible speaks to the "heart" of man—not primarily to the will, moralism, or only to the mind, intellectualism—out of which "is the wellspring of life" (Proverbs 4:23). As Sidney Greidanus observes:

> This Word of God . . . is directed at the heart of man. . . . And the Word addresses man as the religious being he is. This includes undoubtedly the intellect, the will, and the emotions, but not as component parts which must each receive their due. . . . (1970, p. 167)

The Bible is God's witness concerning His mighty acts in the history of redemption. It speaks authoritatively and redemptively to all of life's activities, but it does so with a confessional focus. By "confessional focus" we mean that the Bible, in its total extent and all its parts, witnesses to the heart of man, calling for a faith response to the redeeming work of God in Jesus Christ.

One could, I suppose, focus on other aspects of the Bible, e.g., the political aspects of David's rule, the economic aspects of Solomon's reign, the psychological make-up of Peter, or the lingual aspects of Paul's preaching. But the focus of the Bible is not political, economic, psychological, or lingual—it is confessional. Nor is the Bible, first of all, about David, Solomon, Peter, or Paul—the Bible is about Jesus Christ.

It is also the case that the Bible sometimes focuses on an aspect of creation, e.g., the biotic in the birth of Isaac, the political in the conflict between the Judeans and Samaritans, the aesthetic in the building of the Temple, or the economic in the move of Jacob's family to Egypt. But these are aspects that play a role subservient to the confessional. They are in the Bible to help us understand that God was in Christ reconciling the world to Himself.

Further, an historical-redemptive approach to the teaching of Bible requires that we recognize that God's revelation is *historical*. The Bible is not myth—that which occurs in the arena of the gods—which is why it makes frequent reference to the role of eye-witnesses (Acts 5:32). The Bible is history, i.e., God acts, speaks, and makes man his covenant partner in history. As an historical book the Bible records what God has done for His people. The Bible contains revelation given over a long period of time. Not everything happens at once; God is involved with His people over centuries. Thus, there is an old and new covenant. But from the beginning to the end, the Bible is the history of redemption, always flowing to or from Jesus Christ.

What does this mean for interpretation? It means at least two things. First, it obviously means that we may interpret no passage of the Bible apart from its relationship to Christ. But, second, it means that we must be aware of the time, the revelational epoch, in which a passage of Scripture occurs. For example, we may not interpret Old Testaments laws in the same way we interpret the New Testament command to love one another. This is the point made in "Inspiration and Infallibility," a report to the Synod of the Christian Reformed Church:

> Thus, for example, the Old Testament property laws still instruct us concerning basic principles, but the specific laws governed a situation quite different from ours. This same perspective applies to the New Testament. We no longer feel bound to exchange the holy kiss, to wash one another's feet, or to require women to wear a veil when they pray. Those are exhortations whose form is determined by the culture and circumstances of that time. They still contain an authoritative message for us, but the form of our obedience has been altered by changing circumstances. . . . We interpret the meaning . . . in light of the particular circumstances in which it was addressed. (1972 Agenda, pp. 377, 378)

One more observation in this connection: redemptive history has been written by human writers, which affects the manner in which the divine Word is communicated. There are differences in grammar, style, spirit, and word choice. Further, the writers stand and write from within the history of redemption. They are not mere chroniclers, writing a history of Israel or a biography of Jesus. As writers of redemptive history, inspired by the Holy Spirit, they select events to proclaim what God has done in Christ and what these events mean in God's plan of redemption.

As redemptive history, the revelation in the Bible is *progressive*. There is progress, growth, development in God's revelation, which reaches its fullness in Jesus Christ, the Word become flesh. Deeply imbedded in the history of revelation is the element of teleology, divine purpose.

All this is beautifully explained by Paul K. Jewett as follows:

> There is real forward movement of the hand on the clock of the universe. This is readily seen when we take a larger view of the Old Testament landscape. The basis is laid in the account of the creation of the world and specifically of man, the lord and heir of all he surveys. When he defects from the path of rectitude, God does not cease to act toward him and to speak with him. He seeks out the guilty pair; he clothes their nakedness and though he pronounces a curse upon their heads, it is a malediction big with benediction (Gen. 3:15). And what is this Protevangelium but the promise that God will not cease to act in history till he has destroyed man's mortal foe and undone the mischief which he wrought?
>
> With the lapse of the nations into heathenism, a new start is made in the call of Abraham and the promise that in his seed all the earth shall be blessed (Gen. 12 ff.). This age of the patriarchs is succeeded by that of Moses and the beginning of Israel's national life according to the terms of the Abrahamic Covenant. With the uprooting of Israel from her place in the family of nations, the divine purpose in history is not frustrated; rather, out of the womb of adversity and seeming defeat, the redemptive purpose of God in history emerges enlarged, clarified, spiritualized, the confidence of all the prophets. But the Old Testament idea of history, as the scene of God's acts as Redeemer of his people, is not an end in itself. Its meaning is Jesus Christ, whose name is Emmanuel, God-with-us, who came to "fulfill the law and the prophets." The prophets *had* the Word of God, but Jesus *is* the Word. "And the Word was made flesh and dwelt among us, and we beheld his glory, glory as of the only begotten of the Father, full of grace and truth" (John 1:14). The incarnation is that event in history which gathers up all other revelation into itself. Jesus is the seed of the woman who shall bruise the serpent's head, and when this work shall have been accomplished, then shall the covenant promise be finally fulfilled, then the tabernacle of God shall be with men and he shall be their God and they his people. Thus redemptive history moved from creation to consummation; this is the divine disclosure complete. (1958, pp. 47–48)

As redemptive history, the revelation in the Bible is also *covenantal*. A covenant is a coming together (*con* – with, *venire* – to come) of two persons in fellowship with one another. A covenant may be fellowship between two equals, involving mutual understanding and agreement, e.g., marriage or a business arrangement. It may also be fellowship between two persons who are unequal, with a promise made by one on the basis of a condition to be met by another, e.g., between an employer and employee.

God's revelation in the Bible is covenantal in both senses. God's revelation is based on a covenant between equals—the Father and the Son—in eternity (Psalm 2:7–9). This, the Covenant of Redemption, is basic to God's plan of redemption and the redemptive revelation in the Bible in which we see the plan of God progressively unfolded. God's revelation also makes known the covenant between unequal parties, i.e., between God and the sinner through Jesus Christ. This, the Covenant of Grace, comes from the covenant God to the sinner—a covenantal being—through Jesus Christ, the Mediator of the Covenant (1 Timothy 2:5). The Bible is designed to reveal the provisions of God's covenant with man in Christ, and to bring the sinner into fellowship with God through Jesus Christ. The Bible reveals God as God for us and demands the covenantal response of belief and obedience.

In light of what we have said thus far, the following skeletal outline suggests what courses that teach the Bible in the Christian school should contain:

**Old Testament Revelation**
- A. Creation
  Covenant with Adam
- B. Fall
  Covenant is broken by Adam
- C. First redemptive revelation
  Promise
  Response
  1. Development of sin in line of Cain
  2. Continuity of redemption in line of Seth
- D. Noah to Patriarchs
  1. Flood and Covenant of Nature
  2. Babel and confusion of tongues
- E. Patriarchs
  1. Abraham – Covenant of Grace is formally established
  2. Isaac – restoration of covenant requires offering of human life
  3. Jacob – God is sovereign in transforming life of covenant people

F. Moses
  1. Redemption of covenant people is accomplished
  2. Sinai reveals God as God of a nation
  3. Decalogue reveals way of covenantal obedience
  4. Tabernacle reveals
     - God's presence with His people
     - Sacrifice in atonement for sin
G. Prophets
  1. The office
     - Emerges with the organization of the theocracy under a ruler
     - Commissioned to speak to the ruler as representative of God
  2. Prophets
     - Spoke in the name of the coming Christ
     - Concerned to keep covenant people in fellowship with God through Christ and for the coming of Christ
  3. Prophets present
     - The relationship of God with His people in terms of covenant
     - The effects of sin on the covenant
     - The future in terms of judgment and restoration by grace

**Relationship of the Old and New Testaments**
  A. The unity of the Old and New Testaments
     1. All revelation is the revelation of Jesus Christ
     2. The revelation
        - In the Old Testament looks forward to the New Testament
        - In the New Testament is the fulfillment of the Old Testament
  B. The extent of New Testament revelation
     1. Revelation comes
        - Through Christ directly
        - By Christ through the Apostles
     2. We are now in the New Testament era
     3. Apocalyptic Revelation will occur with the second advent of Christ

**New Testament Revelation**
    A. Nativity – Immanuel, "God with us," comes to restore broken covenant
    B. John the Baptist
        1. Part of the Old Testament dispensation, impatient for coming of Christ
        2. His baptism prepares for the coming of the King
        3. His baptism of Jesus
           - This is He that cometh!
           - Beginning of Christ's ministry
    C. Temptations – Christ is victorious over and begins to bind Satan
    D. Christ's earthly ministry
        1. Regarded Himself and His redemptive work as the fulfillment of the Old Testament
        2. His ministry focused on the Kingdom
        - Comes in the person of the King
        - Reveals divine supremacy in the interest of divine glory
        - Expressed in suffering, death, resurrection, ascension, outpouring of the Holy Spirit
    E. Christ continues His ministry though
        1. The Apostles
        2. The Church

**The Last Days**
    A. The Millennium
    B. Three views concerning the millennium
        1. Premillennialism
        2. Postmillennialism
        3. Amillennialism
    C. An evaluation from a biblical perspective of
        1. Creation
        2. Fall
        3. Redemption
        4. Consummation

**Conclusion**
    A. Jesus Christ is now
        1. Through the ministries of the church as institution—accompanied by the Holy Spirit—expanding, guiding, strengthening, preserving the membership of His Body,

the new humanity
   2. Through the ministries or services of His Body, the new humanity, throughout His creation-kingdom, bringing to expression His kingdom rule
B. Jesus Christ will
   1. Come to claim and glorify the Church, His bride (Ephesians 5:27)
   2. Return the kingdom to His Father, and He will be all in all (1 Corinthians 15:28)

This brings me to the end of my formal presentations. I am not so naïve, however, as to suppose that I have spoken the last word on "Teaching the Bible in the Christian School." I have enjoyed and learned from our discussions but trust that you and your colleagues will continue to discuss what is involved in teaching from a biblical *perspective,* taking time for biblical *devotional* activity, and providing a place in the *academic* program for biblical studies.

God bless you and our Christian schools.

**References**

*Agenda of the synod of the Christian Reformed Church* (1972). Grand Rapids, MI: Christian Reformed Publishing House.

Bouma, C. (1925). *The Bible and Christian education.* Chicago, IL: National Union of Christian Schools.

*Christian Educators Journal,* April, 1971.

Clark, G. H. (November/December 1980). God and Logic. *The Trinity review.*

De Jongste, H. and van Krimpen. (1968). *The Bible and the life of the Christian.* Philadelphia, PA: Presbyterian and Reformed Publishing Co.

DeGraaff, A. (1978). *The nature and aim of Christian education.* Toronto, ON: The Association for the Advancement of Christian Scholarship.

*The Educational Task of Dordt College.* (1979). Sioux Center, IA: Dordt College Press.

Greidanus, S. (1970). *Sola scriptura.* Toronto, ON: Wedge Publishing Foundation.

Jewett, P. K. (1958). Special Revelation as Historical and Personal. In: *Revelation and the Bible.* C. F. H. Henry ed. Grand Rapids, MI: Baker.

Meeter, H. H. (1939). *Calvinism.* Grand Rapids, MI: Zondervan.

Runner, H. E. (1967). *The relation of the Bible to learning.* Hamilton, ON: Guardian Publishing Company Ltd.

*Scripturally-Oriented Higher Education.* (1967). Sioux Center, IA: Dordt College Press.

# Chapter Nine

**To the Reader –**
Shortly after coming to Dordt in 1968, I began to hear discussions about the possibility of starting an agricultural program at the College; and I was privileged to participate in those discussions. From the beginning, there was a mixed response to the idea. Those in favor pointed to the agricultural community in which Dordt is located, observing that it provided an ideal location for such a program. Those opposed insisted that the best place to learn about farming and agriculture was not in college but on the farm.

As the discussions progressed, we began to talk more and more about establishing an Agricultural Stewardship Center, with the emphasis on caring for God's creation—land, plants, and animals—as well as producing food for people: ". . . to work it and take care of it" (Genesis 2:15). Further discussions convinced us that God calls us to be stewards not only of land, plants, and animals, but of His entire creation, i.e., both its *elements* and its *structures*, such as marriage and family, manufacturing, business, civil authority, etc. And, since education is intended to prepare students to work in and to take care of all of the creation, the entire College, with its course of study, should be seen as a Stewardship Center.

It should come as no surprise then, that when Christian Schools International invited me to deliver the 1989 Convention keynote on the subject of "stewardship," I accepted and indicated that my address would be titled, "Educating for Stewardship."

Some years later, in 2005, I delivered one of the convocation addresses in observance of Dordt's 50th anniversary. Reflecting on the fact that a newspaper reporter in Kansas had earlier asked me at a national basketball tournament, "What's a Dordt?" I recalled responding that Dordt College is named after the city of Dordrecht in The Netherlands, where the Canons of Dort with their focus on the sovereignty of God were formulated and adopted, and that Dordt College is a place where students are taught to care for all things that the sovereign God has created and redeemed. Continuing the theme of "stewardship," toward the end of the address, I somewhat facetiously suggested that the College move the sign from the Agricultural Center to the Campus Center and that it read "Dordt College, Academic Stewardship Center." That change hasn't been made as yet; but that's what Dordt College is, a Christian Academic Stewardship Center. Hopefully the following keynote address will explain why I say this.

# Educating for Stewardship

Fellow Stewards:

Thank you for inviting me to speak to you. I always enjoy attending and, whenever asked, addressing these meetings. This is due, in large part, to my belief that you occupy important positions—positions of leadership in the Christian school community.

Thank you also for the subject you have assigned to me, i.e., "Stewards," or "Stewardship." This is a subject of central importance in biblical literature and, also, a subject of contemporary interest and significance. It has been observed, correctly I believe, that the most important issue facing us today "is not the capitalist/communist confrontation, but the war we are all waging on the environment" (*Calvinist Contact*, February 3, 1989, p. 13)—a matter of stewardship. As I prepared this address President Bush, along with seven other world leaders, was meeting in Paris, France. High on the agenda, appropriately, was the issue of the environment.

I'm not certain, however, what you wanted me to consider regarding the broad subject of stewardship. From the correspondence received, I am under the impression that you want me to focus on the good use of God-given talents, efficient scheduling of time, and economic allocation of available funds in the operation of our Christian schools. And, I agree, all of these items must be considered when we talk about stewardship. However, it is also my conviction that, to consider these items correctly, we must view them from a broader perspective and in a larger context. As the authors of *For My Neighbor's Good* have observed:

> The concept of stewardship extends beyond managing the money one has earned (or received). All people are stewards of human life and talents, of time, and of the earth's resources. (Schrotenboer, et al, 1979, p. 29)

Or as Paul Schrotenboer states in *And He had Compassion on Them*, "stewardship is more than thrift, benevolence, or even compassion. It is thankfulness. For Christians it is near to life itself" (1978, p. 44).

---

Keynote, Convention, Christian Schools International, Denver, Colorado, August 1–3, 1989.

Acknowledging that stewardship concerns us all, and desiring to establish a context in terms of which we can rightly consider the use of time, talent, and money, I have developed the thesis for this presentation as follows:

> First, the essence of the Christian's life and the Christian's task in this world is that of stewardship.
>
> Second, it is the responsibility of the Christian school academically to prepare students for their life and/or their task in the world.
>
> Third, therefore, the Christian school is and must be totally involved in the business of stewardship, preparing its students for stewardship.

The task of the Christian school, and our task as stewards, is to prepare covenant youth to be stewards. Therefore, our theme is:

## Educating for Stewardship

Stewardship, as William J. Byron points out in *The Earth is the Lord's*, "is a traditional category . . . associated with people and the creation—given by God to our care and for our use" (1978, p. 45). Commenting on the ethics of stewardship Byron goes on to point out that no one owns anything absolutely, everything we possess we hold in trust; the conditions of that trust are set by the Creator who "entrusts" to our care varying portions of His creation; and the ethic of stewardship concerns itself with fidelity to or violations of that trust.

These observations point us back to the beginning when:

## God Created

The Bible tells us that God, by His Word, brought all things into being—both the heavens and the earth (Genesis 1:1). He then declared that the creation was very good (Genesis 1:31), i.e., capable of fulfilling the purpose for which He made it. It was evident from the beginning that God was creation's God. He was creation's sovereign. The creation belonged to Him.

The Bible tells us, further, that God created the man and the woman in His image (Genesis 1:27). They were part of the creation, yet distinct in the creation. The writers of *Earthkeeping* make this point very clear:

> . . . humans, like stars, seas, whales, fish, and birds are simply a part of creation. . . . humans are also described as being very special in creation, they are made "in the image of God." And they are given a unique position in creation. (1980, p. 208)

According to Genesis 9:9–10, God said to Noah, "I now establish my covenant with you and with your descendants after you and with every living creature . . . on earth." In this covenantal arrangement God calls humans, as He did before, to rule the creation (Genesis 1:28) and to serve the creation, i.e., "to work it and take care of it" (Genesis 2:15). Further, God promised to bless humans and to make the creation flourish when they lived in obedience to His Word. Clearly, God expected humans to care for and keep the earth with as much care as God kept them.

In other words, God charges humans, charges us to be *stewards* of His creation, i.e., "managers of this particular part of his household" (*Earthkeeping,* 1980, p. 224). The Greek term for steward is οἰκονόμος, meaning "manager of the household." It is a term that makes clear that the creation is not ours, it belongs to God (Psalm 24:1); but the creation is entrusted to our care by God. Obedience to God requires faithfulness to that trust. According to Douglas J. Hall in *Imaging God* "To love God is to love and serve his creation. If someone says 'I love God' but hates the creation, that person is a liar" (1986, p. 129).

Further, God made us stewards of the entire creation. This includes not only the *elements* of creation, e.g., water, plants, animals, but also the God-given *structures* of creation, e.g., marriage, family, business, civil authority, etc. In *Earthkeeping* we read:

> . . . the structures of human society are as much a resource as the earth and the sea. In a sense, these resources of human institutions are even more basic to our stewardship of the earth than the earth itself, for it is through them that we affect the earth, for good or for evil. (1980, p. 94)

Which brings us to the sphere of education and the institution of the school. We indeed have a responsibility to be stewards of God's creation. However, given the fact that it is the responsibility of the school to prepare students for the tasks of life, and that those tasks are biblically defined as stewardship, it is clear that the school is called to reflect that responsibility and prepare students to be stewards of the creation. This is true of the entire program of the school—not only courses dealing with environmental issues, but all courses, because both the *elements* and *structures* of creation are to receive stewardly care.

It is interesting to note, in this connection, that the importance of education regarding stewardship is widely recognized today. We recently received a memorandum at Dordt from the White House in which the president of the United States declared that excellence in education requires "environmental sensitivity." In the book, *Meeting the Expectations of the Land,* John Todd states:

. . . there is a vast storehouse of knowledge currently locked up in the insular reaches of academic and scientific institutions which can be used to form a science and practice of . . . stewardship. (1984, p. 156)

In her doctoral dissertation, *Response to Creation,* Ingrid Olsen-Tjensvold writes, "Education is the most powerful incentive to . . . the cause of environmental responsibility" (1980, p. 23).

It's obvious, isn't it, that the school has a manifold responsibility regarding the matter of stewardship. But more of that later. We must now go on to note, in the second place, that after God created:

**Humans Fell**

Created in the image of God, the man/woman were capable of fulfilling their assignment to stewardship. But, tempted by Satan who suggested, "you will be like God," (Genesis 3:5), they broke covenant with God by disobeying His Word. Forgetting that they owned nothing, they violated their trust. Claiming the creation for themselves, they continued to work and care for the creation, but it was in satisfaction of their own desires and not in the service of God.

As a result the judgment of God fell upon the man/woman, humans, and upon the entire creation because of them. The results of the fall were immediately evident in their faith life, as they ran from God (Genesis 3:8); in their marriage, as they dressed themselves and withdrew from one another (Genesis 3:7); and in agriculture, as the ground was cursed to them, producing thorns and thistles (Genesis 3:18).

In this regard the 1989 first-of-the-year issue of *Time* made a tremendous impact on me, and perhaps on some of you as well. Instead of "Person of the Year" the magazine selected the earth as "Planet of the Year." In the following story, the reporters observed:

> For decades, scientists have warned about the reckless way in which humanity has treated its planetary host. No one paid attention.
>
> This year the earth spoke, like God warning Noah of the deluge. Its message was loud and clear, and suddenly people began to listen . . . .
>
> Everyone suddenly sensed that this gyrating globe, this precious repository of all the life that we know of, was in danger. (January 2, 1989, p. 26)

But why? Why is this happening to the earth, to our planet?

Reporting in *The Banner* on a conference titled "Reclaiming the Covenant: Toward a Reformed Theology of Justice, Peace, and the Integrity of Creation," Clifford E. Bajema writes:

> It was indisputably clear to conference participants that the earth faces

a global ecological crisis. And it was also clear to them that the problem stems from human disobedience to God. (Bajema, 1989, p. 8)

Bajema then goes on to describe this crisis as it impacts the *elements* of the creation. The earth's rates of energy transmission are being altered by human acts, such as those causing damage to the ozone layer and the buildup of greenhouse gases. Land, soil, and food production potential are being degraded by growing and dislocated human populations and by increasing demand for goods. Water, both above and below the ground, is becoming increasingly contaminated by synthetic products and by-products. People are destroying forests and habitats, with the result that there are greater floods and more severe droughts. Because their habitats are being destroyed, species of animals and plants are becoming extinct at a rate of more than one species per day. Toxic and radioactive materials, which are continuously being injected into soil, air, and water, are diminishing human life. And human cultures are being displaced, relocated, or extinguished. Artificially concentrated populations undermine the productivity of the land as these populations press for more food and fuel.

Further, there is the crisis that our sin and disobedience have caused relative to the *structures* of creation. In *Creation Regained: Biblical basics for a reformational worldview*, Albert M. Wolters (1985, p. 45) describes many examples of sinful exploitation in this regard when he points to marriage under attack by separation and divorce, family strained by parental neglect, the state twisted by totalitarianism, industry engaged in the waste of environmental resources, corporations and labor unions both driven by naked greed, and academic life corrupted by scientism, sloppy methodology, and fallacious reasoning. All of which makes clear, as we read in *Earthkeeping*,

> . . . that humans are destructively wicked creatures. From Eden on, we have tried to make ourselves gods, and in the attempt we have consistently misused creation. We have always brought pain or death to other persons, and we have as often brought destruction to the wider world . . . . any place or period of our past is filled with examples of such dead-end malignancy; Roman soldiers salting the fields of conquered enemies, Nazis cremating millions of Jews, Americans slaughtering billions of passenger pigeons, the scorched earth policies of a thousand petty tyrants. The contemporary Christian finds in these episodes good reason to despair at the present state of human stewardship and the future prospects for humanity. (De Vos, et al, 1980, p. 5)

In *Imaging God*, John Douglas Hall asks, "What is wrong?" The answer: "We ourselves are wrong. . . . Not just the way we behave, but the way we are" (1986, pp. 6, 10).

In this connection, it is important to note that there are those who hold Christians and Christianity responsible for the plight of the planet. One such Person is Lynn White Jr., author of the well-known article, "The Historical Roots of our Ecological Crisis," which appeared in a 1967 issue of *Science*. White's thesis was that Christianity was responsible for our environmental crisis and that the Christian religion would either have to be revised or abandoned entirely if we were to solve our environmental problems. White based his reasoning on the fact that Christianity teaches that mankind is to have dominion over nature and, therefore, it has treated nature in a destructive way. According to White, Christianity has caused the desacralization of nature and, claiming credit for the development of science and technology, has promoted the very things that have caused our present environmental crisis.

We must confess that there are elements of truth in Professor White's charge. In the name of Christianity much damage has been done to the creation. However, it was a perverted concept of Christianity, which emphasized *ruling* to the neglect of *serving* the creation, i.e., "dressing the garden and keeping it." Francis A. Schaeffer makes much the same point in *Pollution and the Death of Man; The Christian View of Ecology*. Acknowledging elements of truth in White's position, he states:

> However, although this is true, it is not because Christianity does not have the answer, but because we have not acted on the answer . . . . (1970, p. 58)

And then Schaeffer makes a comment that should speak and be of interest to all of us in the reformational community:

> This is an extension of Abraham Kuyper's sphere concept. He sees each of us as many men: the man in the state, the man who is the employer, the man who is the father, the elder in the church, the professor in the university—each of these in a different sphere. But even though they are in different spheres at different times, Christians are to act like Christians *in each of the spheres*. The man is *always* there and he is always a Christian under the norms of Scripture, whether in the classroom or at home. (59)

This is precisely the point that we must emphasize with our students in preparing them to be Christian stewards—as Christians, also in the area of ecology, we are always under the norms of Scripture.

And that leads us, finally, to observe that:

**Christ Redeems**

As we have already indicated, when God *created*, He appointed humans as His representatives, to provide stewardly care for His creation. When these humans fell, deciding to exploit the creation for their own selfish purposes, God visited them and the creation in judgment—the consequences of which we have just described. However, in the fullness of time, God sent His Son into the world to redeem the cosmos, His creation (John 3:16).

It's important to emphasize at this juncture, as Wolters points out in *Creation Regained*, that the redemptive work of Christ involved restoration, "a return to the goodness of the originally unscathed creation"(1985, p. 57). It is even appropriate to speak of Christ's redemptive work as "re-creation." This is not to suggest that the original creation is discarded and that God through Christ brings a new creation into existence; rather, it is to point out that, in covenantal faithfulness, God holds on to the original, fallen creation and restores it in Christ. God will not abandon the work of His hand; in fact, He sacrifices His Son on the cross to reclaim the creation. And humankind, which violated its original assignment, is given a second chance in Christ. We are restored in order that we may, once again, be God's managers, God's stewards on earth.

When Jesus came to earth He fulfilled the true meaning of the Sabbath rest by deeds of helpfulness (Mark 2:28–3:6) and by proclaiming the righteousness of the jubilee year (Luke 4:14–30). By His miracles, Jesus gave us samples of the meaning of restoration by freeing the creation from the bonds of sin and reinstating creaturely living as intended by God. Thus He says to the disciples of John the Baptist: "Go back and report to John what you hear and see: The blind receive sight, the lame walk, men who have leprosy are cured, the deaf hear, the dead are raised and good news is preached to the poor" (Matthew 11:4–5).

Jesus came to restore a fallen and damaged creation! By His death and resurrection He bore the penalty for sin, fulfilled all the requirements of the law, and restored the entire creation, all things in heaven and on earth, to the Father (Colossians 1:20). As the entire creation was brought under the curse of sin, so all of creation was included in the scope of Christ's redemption. One day He will complete the process of restoration. "The creation waits in eager expectation. . ." (Romans 8:19). That expectation will be realized when Christ returns to establish the new heavens and earth wherein will dwell righteousness (Revelation 21).

Meanwhile, we are charged to be stewards of the reclaimed creation. By redeeming us, God has restored us to covenant fellowship with Himself. This restoration is, of course, the result of divine grace; but, it also brings us under obligation—according to the great love command—to be

His representatives and to serve Him as faithful stewards of His creation.

It is sometimes suggested, even stated, that it is our calling in Christ to redeem the creation. Not so! It is only Christ who can and does redeem. It is now our task, as stewards, to bring that redemption to expression, "to promote renewal in every department of creation" (Wolters, 1985, p. 60). And, given the fact that we as educators are to prepare covenant youth for their tasks as stewards of God's creation, this has obvious implications for our Christian schools.

First, it is essential that our educational programs are formed and directed by a reformational worldview. We must avoid a worldview that speaks of a rapture from this cursed earth, that refers to this planet as a "foreign strand," and that allows Christians to wink at the rape of the creation because "heaven is my home." Instead, we must promote and commit to a worldview that acknowledges Christ as the reconciler of all things and understands that we have a ministry of reconciliation in every part of the creation. As Wolters notes:

> Everywhere creation calls for the honoring of God's standards. Everywhere humanity's sinfulness disrupts and deforms. Everywhere Christ's victory is pregnant with the defeat of sin and the recovery of creation. (1985, p. 60)

Second, directed by this biblical, reformational worldview, we must seek to reflect in the school curriculum all aspects of the created order. No part of the creation may be ignored or excluded. Through the curriculum, we must place all aspects of the creation before our students. As we do this, we must together develop a biblical perspective on the creation. Employing the spectacles of the Scripture, we must enable our students to see how the sin of the first Adam has ruined the whole earthly realm and how the redemptive work of the last Adam has restored the entire world. We must also make clear to our students that they, as part of the new humanity, are to promote this restoration. They are to be managers of all the various departments within the creation. Opposing the distortions of sin, they must listen as the entire creation cries out for the loving application of such biblical concepts as reconciliation, sanctification, and renewal.

Third, our students must be made aware of what is happening to both the elements and the structures of creation.

Concerning the *elements* of creation, we must share with students what Eric G. Walther writes in *The Earth is the Lord's*:

> Only in the last one to two hundred years have we developed societies dependent upon the non-renewable fossil fuels of coal, oil, and natural gas. During this brief love affair . . . we have so depleted two of our three

fossil fuels that we must now begin our return to renewable resources. (1978, p. 144)

The renewable resources mentioned are energy forces such as solar energy, wind, hydropower, tides, wood, wave action, and photosynthesis.

We must also call to the attention of students what Joe Paddock, et al., point out in *Soil and Survival*:

> The greatest concentration of prime farmland in the United States—and perhaps in the world—exists in the state of Iowa. After one century of agricultural activity, the topsoil of Iowa is half gone. A frequently quoted description of soil loss tells us that an Iowa farmer, on average, loses two bushels of topsoil for every bushel of corn grown. Some say the loss is really much higher. (1986, p. 7)

Why? Probably because fluctuating political and economic conditions have made farmers more attentive to preserving their way of life than to preserving the soil. In any case, students should be made aware of what is happening to this important element of creation and of their responsibility, as members of the redeemed community of stewards, to reverse this threatening trend.

But they should also be made aware of their responsibility relative to the *structures* of creation. Here again the importance of our reformational worldview should be clearly understood. As Wolters states:

> Marriages should not be avoided by Christians, but sanctified. Emotions should not be repressed, but purified. Sexuality is not simply to be shunned, but redeemed. Politics should not be declared off-limits, but reformed. Art should not be pronounced worldly, but claimed for Christ. Business must no longer be relegated to the secular world, but must be made to conform again to God-honoring standards. (1985, p. 58)

In other words, the students in our classroom must hear the same message heard in a recent conference on "Faith, Science, and the Future" at the Massachusetts Institute of Technology:

> We can say that God values all of creation . . . and that human redemption involves the redemption of the whole cosmos from its "bondage to decay" (Romans 8:18–24). If it is true that human sin has brought evil to the . . . world, so then our acceptance of salvation from sin wrought for us in Christ should show itself in our respective treatment of that world. (Abrecht, 1980, p. 70)

## Conclusion

Our theme for the morning has been "Educating for Stewardship." Does it call us to a proper use of the well-known trio: time, talent, and treasure? Indeed, it does. Does it call us to be stewardly, careful administrators and teachers in our schools? Yes, it does. Does it call us to be role models of stewardship in our personal and professional lives? Of course. But all of this is of quite limited significance unless it is seen in the context of our calling to be stewards in the field of education, preparing our students to prepare to care for every part of our Father's redeemed but still hurting world.

Or, as Christian ecologist Cal De Witt has stated, we must prepare our students to live and work on this earth, so that living and working in the new earth will not be too much of a shock!

**References**

Abrecht, P. (1980). *Faith and science in an unjust world.* Paul Abrecht, ed. Philadelphia, PA: Fortress Press.

Bajema, C. E. (April 3, 1989). "Reclaiming the Covenant: Toward a Reformed Theology of Justice, Peace, and the Integrity of Creation. *The Banner*, 124

Byron, W. J. (1978). The Ethics of Stewardship. In *The earth is the Lord's.* Marilyn E. Jegen and Bruno V. Manno, eds. New York: Paulist Press.

De Vos, P., et al. (1980). *Earthkeeping: Christian stewardship of natural resources.* Loren Wilkinson, ed. Grand Rapids, MI: Eerdmans.

Hall, D. J. (1986). *Imaging God: Dominion as stewardship.* Grand Rapids, MI: Eerdmans.

Hielema, B. (February 3, 1989). Reclaiming the covenant. *Calvinist Contact*, 44.

Olsen-Tjensvold, I. (1980). *Response to creation.* Ann Arbor, MI: University of Michigan.

Paddock, J. et al. (1986). *Soil and survival.* San Francisco, CA: Sierra Club Books.

Sancton, T. A. (January 2, 1989). Planet of the year. *Time*, 71.

Schaeffer, F. A. 1970. *Pollution and the death of man.* Wheaton IL: Tyndale House Publishers.

Schrotenboer, P., et al. (1978). *And he had compassion on them.* Grand Rapids, MI: Board of Publications of the Christian Reformed Church.

Schrotenboer, P., et al. (1979). *For my neighbor's good.* Grand Rapids, MI: Board of Publications of the Christian Reformed Church.

Todd, J. (1984). The Practice of Stewardship. In *Meeting the expectations of the land.* Wes Jackson, Wendell Berry, and Bruce Colman, eds. San Francisco, CA: North Point Press.

Walther, E. G. (1978). Stewardship and the Food, Energy, Environment Triangle. In *The earth is the Lord's.* Mary Evelyn Jegen and Bruno V. Manno, eds. New York: Paulist Press.

White, L. Jr. (1967). The historical roots of our ecological crisis. *Science*, 155.

Wolters, A. M. (1984). *Creation regained: Biblical basics for a reformational worldview.* Grand Rapids, MI: Eerdmans.

# Chapter Ten

**To the Reader —**

Two keynote addresses on "creativity." What a challenge! Why?

First, this was a new subject for me. Even though it seemed interesting and worthwhile, it would require a great deal of work and research. Second, my presentations were to serve as keynote addresses, providing the groundwork for the "sectionals" that were to follow. And, since many of the sectional leaders were experts in the area of creativity, I wanted to make sure that my work would, indeed, serve its purpose. Third, some of the sectional leaders were highly creative members of Dordt's faculty (one of them, art instructor Joanne Alberda, was from Manhattan, Montana where the convention was being held) and I certainly did not want to make it necessary for them to apologize for the performance of their president.

In light of the above, you may wonder why I accepted this challenge. The reason is quite simple. Prior to this time, in faculty meetings at the college, we had been talking about ways in which we could be of ongoing service and support to the larger Christian school community, especially to the graduates of Dordt's teacher education program. (It was about this time, and for this purpose, that we began the Center for Educational Services, under the direction of Dr. John Van Dyk.) Therefore, when I noted that a number of the members of the Convention Planning Committee had Dordt connections, I was quick to accept.

The fact that many of the convention sectional leaders were members of the Dordt faculty was actually very helpful in my preparation. It gave me an opportunity to contact them directly, learn from them, and bounce many of my untested ideas off of them. They were very patient with me and also very helpful to me. I should say that the strengths of what I had to offer were due in large part to their insights and suggestions, while the weaknesses and inconsistencies were totally my responsibility.

One more observation: I was asked to present two keynotes on the general topic of "creativity." This was not easy, but after some thought, I decided to speak on "Christian Education and Creativity" in two parts: 1) Creator, Creature, Creativity and 2) Creativity, a Kingdom Activity. The two parts are presented as one in the following.

# CHRISTIAN EDUCATION AND CREATIVITY

Colleagues in the work of Christian Education:

Thank you for inviting me to keynote this convention on "Creativity, Being and Becoming." Frankly, I don't know why you invited me to speak on this topic. I have not spoken on creativity before. I certainly am no expert on the subject. Further, I'm not certain as to why I accepted your invitation. Perhaps it was because I saw this as an opportunity to give focused attention to the study of this important subject and to learn even more from listening to your discussion during the next few days.

You will notice that I'm speaking on "Christian Education and Creativity," not just creativity in general or in the abstract, but creativity as it relates to Christian education. Obviously, I chose this title because I was invited by and am speaking to men and women involved, as I am, in the work of Christian education.

**Introduction**

The subject of creativity has been of interest since ancient times. The Greek philosophers dealt quite extensively with creativity. Plato, for example, equated creativity with divine inspiration and suggested that the creative person is "out of his mind" during the creative process. Aristotle, on the other hand, rejected such supernatural involvement and insisted that creativity occurred spontaneously or by chance.

Until recently, however, the interest in creativity has been quite detached from other matters, and the subject of creativity has been dealt with in a rather abstract manner. But since 1950—in the United States, at least—potential competition with other countries has spurred the attempts to improve knowledge, conquer the unknown, and create new ideas and new things. This increased interest, according to Calvin W. Taylor, has opened many avenues of research and has produced a flood of articles and books on the subject of creativity (1964, p. 2).

In reviewing the literature on the topic of creativity, it is interesting to note that frequent reference is made to the importance of education.

---

Keynote, Convention, Christian Schools International, District 11, Manhattan, Montana, October 15–17, 1986.

In *Creativity: Progress and Potential*, for example, there is a chapter by E. Paul Torrance, titled "Education and Creativity" (Taylor, 1964, p. 50). Torrance indicates that education is legitimately interested in creativity because it is concerned with fully functioning persons, mental health, educational achievement, vocational success, and the general well-being of society.

If it is true that education is legitimately interested in creativity—and I believe it is true—then especially Christian educators should be interested and involved in the issue of creativity. It is to demonstrate the truth of this statement that I wish now to speak to you about *Christian Education and Creativity*.

**Creator**

When we think of creativity as Christian educators, we must think first of God, the Creator. There continues to be much discussion in the church concerning creation versus evolution. This is an important discussion that certainly should interest all those involved in Christian education. However, in the midst of this discussion, we must not lose our focus. As we discuss such issues as days versus long periods of time, macro and micro evolution, and gaps in the fossil record we must be careful lest we forget the most important issue, i.e., that God and God alone is the Creator.

In Genesis 1:1, do we read "In the beginning *man* engaged in creative activity"? No, but "In the beginning *God* created the heavens and the earth." The focus is on God the Creator, not on human creative activity. The work of creating was a free act of the triune God, who created partly out of nothing and partly out of existing material. Creation was initiated by the Father through the agency of the Son and the ordering, life-giving activity of the Holy Spirit.

In the Bible, we read that God saw everything that He had created, "and it was very good" (Genesis 1:31). That which God made was "good" because it fulfilled the purpose for which it was made, namely, His praise and glory. When we consider the creative work of God—light and dark, water and land, vegetation, the planets and stars, animals on the land and fish in the sea, angels, man and woman—we see that it was all good. The creation was not a confusing chaos, but an ordered cosmos. It was one grand unity, existing in an exciting diversity. It presented a marvelous picture, unmarred by sin. When the writer of Psalm 19 beholds the creation he exclaims, "The heavens declare the glory of God; the skies proclaim the work of his hands" (Psalm 19:1). Glorious! That is the only word that can even begin to describe God's creation. It is something in which He delights, and so should we.

**Creatures**

The result of the Creator's activity is called the "creation." God, the Creator, is the source, the preserver, and the governor of the creation. All things in God's creation are "creatures." They are called creatures because they are the result of His creative activity and dependent on Him for their continuing creaturely existence.

But, there is one of God's creatures that stands out above all the rest; that one is "man," a human being, created "in the image of God" (Genesis 1:27). Created in the image of God. What does that mean? It does not mean that the human person does as a creature what God did or does at the divine Creator. It does not mean that as God thinks, so the human thinks; as God speaks, so the human speaks; or as God works, so the human works. Nor does it mean that as God created, so the human creates (Seerveld, 1980, pp. 26–27).

To take the position that "in the image of God" means that the creature is able to do what the Creator did, blurs the distinction between the Creator and the creature—turning the human into a little god and God into nothing more than a big human being—which is contrary to the biblical teaching, which makes clear that God, the Creator, is distinct from that which is created and creaturely. In Job 37:14–18, for example, we read:

> Listen to this, Job;
>   stop and consider God's wonders.
> Do you know how God controls the clouds
>   and makes his lightning flash?
> Do you know how the clouds hang poised,
>   those wonders of him who is perfect in knowledge?
> You who swelter in your clothes
>   when the land lies hushed under the south wind,
> can you join him in spreading out the skies,
>   hard as a mirror of cast bronze?

Job's response is clear: "I am unworthy—how can I reply to you? It put my hand over my mouth" (Job 40:4).

The essence of the human being "in the image of God" is found in the concept of "representation." "In the image of God means that the human being—in distinction from other creatures—is God's representative in the creation":

> The idea of representation refers to man in the concreteness and visibility of his earthly life; to man, who was created in God's image and likeness and who is called to represent and portray this image here on earth . . . . This concept deals with man as he actually is, the non-autonomous and non-independent creature, unable to rely on himself alone; man, who can find and possess his riches and his glory precisely only in his dependence on and in his communion with God. (Berkouwer, 1962, p. 114)

But what is the human being to do as God's image-bearer? What is he or she to do as God's representative? To answer that question we move on to consider creativity.

## Creativity

There is something we should note about God's good creation, i.e., it was not to remain as it was in the beginning. True, in the beginning the creation was good, beautiful, and unmarred by sin. But, as a flower it was to grow, first the bud and then the full bloom; and as a treasure it was to be discovered, uncovered, and displayed for all to see. Thus, as God gave creation a beginning, so He would give it a history in which the creation would develop full-grown according to the purpose and unto the praise of its Creator.

To that end, God made a covenant with His creation promising that, if the creation was obedient, He would bless the creation. At the same time, God determined to realize this covenant through His human representatives. God made the male and female in His image, and He gave to them as His representatives what has come to be called the "cultural mandate":

> Be fruitful and increase in number; fill the earth and subdue it. Rule over the fish of the sea and the birds of the air and over every living creature that moves on the ground. (Genesis 1:28)

and

> The Lord God took the man and put him in the Garden of Eden to work it and take care of it. (Genesis 2:15)

The cultural mandate indicated that the man and the woman, as cultural agents, were placed in the creation with the responsibility to develop God's creation. They were to bring that flower to full bloom; they were to discover, uncover, and display that glorious treasure.

In *The Creativity Question* Albert Rothenberg and Carl Hausman describe creative activity in terms of *newness* and *value* (1976, p. 1). That which creative activity produces is new in that it is of increased complexity; and it is valuable, a thing of worth and usefulness, in that it marks an advancement or improvement on that which has preceded it. Accepting the truth of this description, we can say that when God presented the man and woman with the cultural mandate, He was calling upon His image-bearing creatures to work creatively with His creation.

Taking another approach, in *Intelligence, Creativity, and Their Educational Implications*, J. P. Guilford (1968) describes divergent thinking, which is associated with creativity, in terms of the following: *fluency*, coming up with a large number of ideas, words, or expressions; *flexibility*, developing new ways to deal with issues; *originality* producing clever, novel ideas; and *elaboration*, adding additional items to a response. This indeed is what is meant by creativity. A creative person is one who is curious, questioning, imaginative, and inventive. Creativity is the ability to bring about something new, original.

When God made the man and woman in His image, He made them capable of being His representatives and of working creatively with His creation. When God told them to "rule over" the creation, to "work it and care for it," He was commanding them to develop His creation, to work creatively with the stuff of His creation—bringing out of the creation that which was *new* and of *value*, that which reflected *fluency*, *flexibility*, *originality*, and *elaboration*.

What we have observed up to this point means at least four things concerning creativity. First, all of God's human creatures—by virtue of their creation in the image of God—are capable of creativity. Creative ability is not something reserved for a select few. It is something that is possessed by and is to be developed in all of us, especially in our students. H. H. Rookmaaker recognized this:

> Creative activity is nothing special . . . . When we speak about creativity, we do not mean only art. Creativity is part of everyone's work, wherever the best solution to a task is sought in love and freedom. This applies both to our contribution to social relationships and to our specific work in engineering, in science, in theology—where things have to be made or problems solved. (1981, p. 74)

Second, creativity is good. In the past, some have been inclined to view creativity as something frivolous and wasteful. Not so. Creativity is good because it is commanded by God and, therefore, it is to be encouraged by us, especially by us as teachers in working with our students.

Third, creativity involves work. God commands us to work creatively with the creation. It is sometimes suggested that one must wait for creativity or that creativity just happens. There is no doubt that there can be and are moments of creative inspiration; but, as the inventor Thomas

A. Edison observed, creativity is far more perspiration than inspiration. David Perkins makes the same point in *Educational Leadership,* when he states that creativity "depends on working at the edge . . . of one's competence" (September 1984, p. 19).

Fourth, creativity finds its fulfillment in praise to God. Too many creative people work hard to bring praise to themselves. The Bible instructs us that we are to live creatively in the service and praise of our God. Edith Schaeffer (1971, p. 82) says it well when she observes that our creativity "should reflect something of the artistry, the beauty and order of the One" whom we represent and in whose image we have been made.

This fourth item—that creativity finds its fulfillment in praise to God—leads us to observe that creativity is kingdom activity.

## Kingdom Activity

When God created the heavens and the earth, He brought into existence His kingdom. God is the originator of the creation who preserves and governs the creation. The creation belongs to God, is governed by the Word or law of God, and exists to serve God. In other words, the creation is the kingdom of God. That is why H. Evan Runner (1968, p. 31) writes, "Everything in heaven and on earth is subject to Him; for He is the Creator. His ordinances rule the heavenly bodies (Psalm 119:89–91); the earth also is His possession" (Psalm 2). And that is what Abraham Kuyper was talking about, at the founding of the Free University of Amsterdam in 1880, when he asserted that there is not one square inch of creation concerning which God does not say, "It is mine."

The man and woman, image-bearing creatures of God, were made to be citizens of the kingdom. They were to serve the kingdom, and they were qualified for that service by virtue of being created in the image of God. And how were the man and the woman to serve the kingdom? By working creatively, as we have already pointed out, as God's representatives in discovering, uncovering, and displaying the wonders of the created order. All of which means that creativity is kingdom activity and, because creativity is kingdom activity, it is subject to the law of God, the King of the kingdom.

In a recent work, titled *Responsible Technology,* the authors observe that

> As image bearers of God, human beings are responsible before God for their activities. They are accountable for the way they exercise their creativity: what they do with their lives, what and how they shape, mold, and form. God has established a law by which men and women are expected to live. (Monsma, et al., 1986, p. 38)

It is important to emphasize this because today we are living with a Greek notion of creativity. The ancient Greeks held that creativity was due to the direct operation of the gods. For example, Plato believed that poets performed their craft by the inspiration of some divine power and, therefore, poets were to be elevated above others. They were not subject to the laws and rules of mere mortals. They were a law unto themselves. What they did was right because they did it.

We still tend to think that creative ability marks someone as special. A creative person is a law unto himself or herself and is not subject to the rules and regulations that must be observed by others. This is not so, of course. Creative activity is kingdom activity, i.e., activity that is for the King and subject to His will, His law.

At first the man and woman did perform their creative work in obedience to the Word of God. In light of the Word, they sought to understand the creation. According to the Word, they endeavored to work creatively with the creation. In that way, the man and woman served the King and advanced the cause of the kingdom.

But then Satan entered the picture and—by trying to wipe out the Creator/creature distinction—tempted the man and woman to disobey the law and Word of God. They fell. After the fall into sin, they were still creatures of God, retained the image of God, and continued to work creatively in the creation. But now, there were two kinds of creativity. There was obedient creativity, but there was also disobedient creativity.

Because of sin, there was creativity that disobeyed the Word of God and sought to advance the kingdom of this world for the praise of humans. Think, for example, of Jabel, the father of those who dwell in tents and have cattle; Jubal, the father of all those who play the lyre and the pipe; and Tubal-Cain, the forger of all instruments of bronze and iron (Genesis 4:19–22). All of these persons, by virtue of God's common grace, worked creatively (Meeter, 1939, p. 86). In fact, they outworked the children of God in this regard. But they did their work to advance self and the kingdom of this world. That's why Lamech, their father, arrogantly sings in Genesis 4:23–24:

> Adah and Zillah, listen to me;
>   wives of Lamech, hear my words.
> I have killed a man for wounding me,
>   a young man for injuring me.
> If Cain is avenged seven times,
>   then Lamech seventy-seven times.

There is also creativity that obeys the Word of God and seeks to advance the kingdom of God for His praise. Such creativity was made possible, however, only through the redemptive work of Jesus Christ—promised by God already in Genesis 3:15. By the death and resurrection of His Son, God reclaimed the creation as His kingdom and redeemed His elect sons and daughters as citizens of that kingdom. As restored image-bearers, the redeemed are to represent God. They are made responsible to care for His creation-kingdom. They are called to serve creatively in the kingdom, to obey the King's laws, and to advance His kingdom.

Because the redemptive work of Christ has significance for the kingdom community today, it obviously has tremendous significance for Christian education.

**Christian Education**

Usually when asked concerning the purpose of Christian education, we respond by saying that it is to prepare young people for service in the kingdom of God. In light of what has been presented up to this point regarding creativity, we could just as well say that it is the purpose of Christian education to nurture the creative abilities of our young people and thus to prepare them for creative service and activity in the kingdom.

In this connection, the first thing to observe is that creativity can be nurtured. It can even be taught! Writing specifically about creative thinking, Sidney Parnes and Arnold Meadow observe:

> The study of creativity is far too immature to make certain exactly what happens in a person who studies and practices the principles of creative thinking. We feel that it is a combination of attitude and ability development. But our recent research does seem to warrant the postulate that the gap between an individual's innate creative talent and his lesser actual creative output can be narrowed by deliberate education in creative thinking. (1963, p. 320)

Some have suggested that creativity should be taught as a new subject or skill. Others advise modification of the school curriculum so that we may draw upon the creative potential in all the subject matter we treat. I am inclined, along with George F. Kneller, to prefer the latter course.

> First, we know as yet too little about creativity to teach it effectively on its own . . . . Second, and more important, creativity is not an isolated process but a component of many kinds of activity . . . if a person is to make full use of his talents, he should learn to think creatively in a range of situations and on a variety of subjects. (1965, pp. 77–78)

Kneller moves on to indicate how creativity can be nurtured and taught. He states that our educational programs should encourage originality, appreciation of the new, inventiveness, curiosity and inquiry, self-direction, and sense perception. At the same time, Kneller issues a significant warning:

> Although in the past education has neglected creativity, it would be folly to go to the opposite extreme and extol it to the detriment of mental discipline and mastery of subject matter . . . . for successful creation demands both material for the imagination to work on and techniques for transforming that material into realized form. (1965, p. 88)

Exactly how to nurture and educate for creativity is a complicated matter that cannot be adequately described or dealt with in a presentation such as this. One is reminded of the complicated nature of this matter when studying the work of persons such as E. Paul Torrence, an educational psychologist quoted earlier, and J. P. Guilford, author of the well-known book, *The Nature of Human Intelligence* (McGraw-Hill, Inc., 1967). At the same time, I do wish to note briefly some guidelines for our Christian schools so that we may promote the God-given creative potential in the lives of our students.

Before doing so, however, we must admit that formal education typically tends to hinder creativity:

> The negative attitude toward creativity begins with our system of education and never ends. When I was a little boy in school a long, long time ago I used to get rapped on the knuckles with a ruler for writing with my left hand. The early lesson here: don't be different.
>
> Today our educational institutions are still dedicated to standardization and regularity. (McCabe, 1985, p. 630)

Obviously, there is "too little imagination and creativity in educational institutions" (Ahrell, 1983, p. 101). Therefore, we must work hard in our Christian schools to rid ourselves, first, of the attitude that is bothered or threatened by creative and inquisitive children; second, of the idea that learning can take place only in the tightly structured classroom; third, of the approach to learning that allows little alternative thought or inquiry; and fourth, of the notion that creativity is limited to music, literature, drama, and art—having nothing to do with other subjects or other aspects of learning. At the same time, we must introduce and encourage things that promote creativity. As Donald W. MacKinnon states:

> It is our task as psychologists and educators either through our insights or through the use of validated predictors to discover talent when it is still potential and to provide that kind of social climate and intellectual environment which will facilitate its development and expression. (1952, p. 484)

As to guidelines for promoting the creative potential of our students, we must first encourage creative children. Keith F. Kennett, who describes creativity in terms of "divergent thinking" as opposed to "convergent thinking," points out that this can be done when teachers become "helpers as well as directors." They must provide classroom experiences that ensure the enjoyment of understanding; encouragement of independence, self-reliance, and responsibility; availability of opportunities to initiate inquiry; and development of competencies that allow for contrast and avoid forcing children into a mold (1984, p. 5).

Second, instead of structuring the classroom so tightly that creativity is choked off, we must seek to create an atmosphere that includes a sound, healthy, secure climate; incentives for inventiveness; tolerance for diversity with and among students; and adequate cultural resources, such as music, books, art, and field trips to exciting places. It is important in this regard to avoid extremes: We must not structure the classroom so that creativity is destroyed; nor must we promote creativity to the extent that we lose control of the classroom. As Torrance indicates we must promote creativity "while maintaining control" (1964, p. 91). Admittedly, that is not easy. One obvious prerequisite is that our control or discipline must be both "consistent and predictable" (MacKinnon, 1962, p. 492).

Third, instead of a narrow approach to learning, we must introduce a spirit of adventure into the classroom. And that should not be difficult for us as Christian educators. Our God, the Creator of the heavens and the earth, is a great God who always guides us by His Word. The creation is vast, filled with rich and exciting diversity. And the children whom we are preparing for service in that creation-kingdom are naturally creative. According to James Alvino:

> Creative behaviors begin at birth and increase up to about age 6 or 7. During these crucial years, children are eager to be original and discover on their own. If they are suppressed or ridiculed during this time, the joy of creative activities is likely to be replaced by apathy or guilt. (1984, p.48)

Finally, instead of limiting creativity to certain courses, we must seek to promote creativity in every class for every child, because creativity is an ability given by God to all children to be used in every aspect of their lives. Doing so we must recognize, as Robert Alexander states, that the natural behavior of children

> . . . is to create, to allow the unconscious to bring into being shapes, sounds, forms and colors of flowers, trees, mountains . . . the fantastic symphony that is life. As children create their imaginations are alive, vi-

brant, and fully operative . . . they are seriously and joyously embarking on a journey of exploration and discovery. (1984, p. 478)

Recently I received a letter asking if there is "a course or a section of a course on creativity" in the curriculum of Dordt College. I answered by indicating that we do not have a particular course on creativity, but that there are sections of certain courses where creativity is extensively considered. In responding to this letter I was reminded in a very direct manner that, also on the college level, it is important to encourage creativity not simply by means of one course, but throughout the entire academic program (Torrance, 1964, p. 125).

**Concluding Summary**
In the beginning God brought forth the creation as His kingdom. He made humans in His image to work creatively in obediently developing the creation. When they fell into sin, humans continued to work creatively, but they did so disobediently. Through the redemptive work of Jesus Christ, God reclaimed the creation as His kingdom and now calls His redeemed sons and daughters to work creatively for Him in advancing His kingdom. It is the task of Christian education on all levels to reflect that kingdom and academically to prepare young people for kingdom service. Therefore, as Christian educators, we not only may, but we must nurture the creative ability of our students.

**References**
Ahrell, R. (November 1983). Educational leadership: Key to encouraging creativity. *The Clearing House,* 57.
Alexander, R. (September 1984). What are children doing when they create? *Language Arts,* 61.
Alvino, J. (May 1984). Nurturing children's creativity and critical thinking skills. *The Educational Digest,* 49.
Berkouwer, G. C. (1962). *Man: the image of God.* Grand Rapids, MI: Eerdmans.
Guilford, J. P. (1968). *Intelligence, creativity, and their educational implications.* San Diego: R. R. Knapp.
Kennett, K F. (Fall 1984). Creativity: Educational necessity for modern society. *Education* 105.
Kneller, G. F. (1965). *The art and science of creativity.* New York: Holt, Rhinehart, and Winston, Inc.
MacKinnon, D. W. (July 1962). The nature and nurture of creative talent. *American Psychologist,* 17.
McCabe, E. A. (July 15, 1985). Creativity. *Vital Speeches,* 51.
Meeter, H. H.. (1939). *Calvinism: An interpretation of its basic ideas.* Grand Rapids, MI: Zondervan.

Monsma, S. V., et al. (1986). *Responsible technology.* Stephen V. Monsma, ed. Grand Rapids, MI: Eerdmans.

Parnes, S. J. and M., A. (1963). Development of individual creative talent. In Calvin W. Taylor and Frank Barron, eds. *Scientific creativity, its recognition and development.* New York: John Wiley and Sons, Inc.

Perkins, D. (Sept. 1984). Creativity by design. *Educational Leadership,* 42.

Rookmaaker, H. H. (1981). *The creative gift.* Westchester, IL: Cornerstone Books.

Rothenberg, A. and Hausman, C. (1976). The creative question. In Albert Rothenberg and Carl Hausman, eds. *The creative question.* Durham, NC: Duke University Press.

Runner, H. E. (1968). *The Bible and the life of the Christian.* Philadelphia, PA: Presbyterian and Reformed Publishing Co.

Schaeffer, E. (1971). *Hidden art.* Wheaton, IL: Tyndale House Publishers.

Seerveld, C. (1980). *Rainbows for the fallen world.* Downsview, ON: Toronto Tuppence Press.

Taylor, C. W. (1964). Introduction. In: *Creativity: Progress, and potential.* Calvin W. Taylor, ed. New York: McGraw-Hill.

Torrance, E. P. (1964). Education and creativity. In: *Creativity: Progress and potential.* Calvin W. Taylor, ed. New York: McGraw-Hill.

# CHAPTER ELEVEN

**To the Reader –**

Dr. Sung Soo Kim was director of the teacher education program at Kosin University, a Christian institution of higher education in Busan, South Korea. Late in the 1980's, he contacted Dordt about the possibility of spending time in the college's Studies Institute. He indicated that he had heard about Dordt and its reformational perspective and wanted to observe how that perspective came to expression in the curriculum—especially in the Education Department. Having been accepted, Dr. Kim moved with his wife and two children to Sioux Center and spent a significant amount of time in the Studies Institute and attending classes to observe how Dordt, as indicated in its purpose statement, seeks to permeate all the students' intellectual, emotional, and imaginative activities with the spirit and teachings of the Reformed, Christian faith.

Following his return to South Korea, Dr. Kim invited me, as well as others from Dordt, to speak at Kosin University. I had been privileged to speak earlier at the celebration of the 50th Anniversary of Kosin and the establishment of the official relationship between Kosin and Dordt College. On this occasion, however, I was asked to speak to the Association of Christian Teachers Society, meeting at Kosin University. The assigned topic was "Preparing Christian Teachers for the Future." Following my presentation, which was translated into Korean, Dr. Kim asked if I would speak on the same subject the following morning to his class of Christian public school teachers. When I agreed to do so, he pointed out that most of the Kosin graduates taught in public schools and that, while I should make basically the same presentation I did to the Christian Teachers Society, I should focus more on the future of the teachers than that of the schools.

Of course, I followed Dr. Kim's advice. The classroom lecture was well-received and resulted in a lively discussion. It proved to be a rich educational experience for me and, according to reports, for the students as well. Actually, it alerted me to the importance of discussions in teacher education departments at Dordt and in other institutions of Christian higher education about how to prepare students to teach as Christians in public as well as in Christian schools.

# Preparing Christian Teachers for the Future

There is much talk today about the future, especially since we're moving closer to the year 2000 (Y2K), the end of the 20$^{th}$ and the beginning of the 21$^{st}$ century. This talk has spilled over into the academy, with courses focusing on the future. Already in the early 70s, my graduate program included a course on the Sociology of the Future.

It's difficult to talk about the future. For one thing, we don't know much—if anything—about the future. In addition, we live in a fast-changing society, which makes the future uncertain. Just one example: In 1994 our children, in recognition of forty years in the ministry, gave me a contemporary, up-to-date world globe. Today, just three years later, that globe is quite out-of-date as a result of national boundary changes we could not have predicted.

So, what shall we do with our topic, *Preparing Christian Teachers for the Future*? In response to that question, I'm suggesting that we consider this in light of what we judge to be the spirits operative in our society today. I realize that those of us present here today are living and working in different countries and different cultures—and that includes your speaker. Still, my reading and experience suggest that our countries and cultures share important characteristics in common, characteristics that will universally impact the future and how we should prepare for the future, including the future of Christian teachers and Christian education.

The spirits operative in contemporary society indicate that preparing Christian teachers for the future requires that these teachers:

## Be Committed Christians

Our society has been characterized as a pluralistic, postmodern society. As religiously pluralistic, society is open to a wide variety of faiths and worldviews. While modernism was intellectually certain about ev-

---

Presentation in South Korea to a meeting of the Association of Christian Teachers Society, and a class of Christian public school teachers at Kosin University, October 1997.

erything, our postmodern society is hesitant to be certain about anything. In this spirit, postmodern pluralism recognizes Christianity as one of many faiths and worldviews; but, in relativistic fashion, it goes on to insist that Christianity is neither more right or wrong than any other religion. Actually, considering all the options available, it's not so important what you believe, just so long as you believe something.

In this climate, and faced with this type of challenge, it's obviously important for the Christian to be committed and consistently willing to profess, "I know whom I have believed" (2 Timothy 1:12). The Christian is someone who trusts in God the Father as the Creator, Christ as the only Savior, and the indwelling Holy Spirit alone as qualifying him/her for Christian service.

However, this type of commitment is needed not only of Christians in general, but also and especially of Christians living and working in the sphere of education. Christian education is Christ-centered education, which means that Christian teachers must acknowledge the exclusive claim of Christ: "I am the way and the truth and the life. No one comes to the Father except through me" (John 14:6). This does not mean that Christian teachers should not teach their students about other religions, note similarities to Christianity in other religions, or express appreciation for elements to be found in other faiths. But, in the end, Christian teachers must be committed to maintaining the exclusive right of Christ to claim, "I am the light of the world" (John 8:12). The moment we are willing to compromise on this commitment, we run the risk of losing the right to claim that the instruction we provide is Christian.

So much for your Christian commitment. Now a word about your job, your position as Christian teachers. It is important that you:

**Hold to a Biblical Concept of Office**

Our society, as you know, is very job-conscious. Young people view education primarily as a means to obtaining a lucrative job. Adults are concerned with looking for, obtaining, keeping, and advancing to a high paying job. Because of this, American politicians often conduct their campaigns for election or re-election on promises of jobs, jobs, and more jobs.

No one will deny that it is important to have a job and to make enough money to support one's self and, in many cases, one's family. However, it is even more important that Christians—also and especially in their jobs—have a sense of calling, a consciousness of office, i.e., an awareness of for whom and for what purpose they do their work. The biblical concept of office answers these questions, informing us as to how God uses people, His redeemed people, to administer the affairs of His creation.

In the beginning God placed the man, the woman—His image-bearers—over the rest of creation to administer the creation-kingdom in His service and according to His Word. This was their calling, task, office from and for God. Through the fall into sin, the man and woman failed to fulfill their office. Jesus Christ was graciously appointed to be their substitute servant, office-bearer. As suffering servant, He performed the work of redemption by atoning for sin and meeting the demands of the Word of God. As glorified office-bearer, He has been given the authority to administer the affairs of the restored creation-kingdom of God.

Jesus Christ administers the affairs of the creation-kingdom through people, especially the redeemed people of God. All of the redeemed have a calling, task, office as servants of Christ. At the same time, there are particular, special offices to which the redeemed are called. And, as Calvin Seerveld points out in "Cultural Objectives for the Christian Teacher," office involves "the position of authority" one exercises in a certain area, "authority granted by God" (Seerveld, n.d., p. 16).

One such area is that of education. In the area or sphere of education the teacher has a calling, task, office from Christ that is to be performed humbly in dependence upon Christ, obediently according to His Word, and confidently with authority from Christ. The teacher does not receive authority from parents, church, government, or society in general—even though he or she must be sensitive to the wishes and needs of people in those areas. The teacher receives authority from Christ and must work with students according to the Word and for the sake of the kingdom of Christ, for Christ is the One who has called him or her to the office of teacher.

Responding to the call of Christ, the Christian teacher must:

**Reflect a Sense of Community**

Our age is an age of individualism. Individualism isolates people from one another. The Bible calls us to think of individuals in community, that is, to acknowledge that God created and recreated us to live and work in community.

In *Man in God's World* Paul Schrotenboer reflects on the biblical idea of office. Doing so, he writes:

> . . . we understand that the basic idea of office is that God appoints man to perform a certain task communally. As man sought to perform this

task, he developed the social machinery which now characterizes our highly organized multi-zoned life. (1972, p. 18)

In other words, in the beginning the human community was undifferentiated, and performed all of its tasks within the context of the family. As these tasks became more complex and the offices more specialized, differentiation occurred. As a result, task communities emerged in addition to the family, such as the church, state, and industry.

One of these task communities is the school, which functions in close relationship with other task communities. There are also task communities within the school, such as administrators, students and teachers. As the authors of *A Vision with a Task* note:

> We are called to a life of discipleship, personally and communally. Christian schools must become living examples of Chris-confessing communities. They must operate in ways that enable students and teachers to unfold the gifts that they have been given. They must develop ways of sharing each other's joys and burdens, looking out for the interests of others. (1993, p. 106)

Christian teachers must have a kingdom vision that makes them aware of the communal context of the Christian school. They must be aware of the relationship of the school to other task communities, especially the family and the church. They must also sense and confess the communion of the saints within the school, which makes them aware of their relationship to administrators, students, and other teachers and of the importance of working together in a spirit of harmony with, dependence upon, and support for one another. Only in this way can they avoid the pitfalls of individualism and accomplish the task to which they have been called.

Having a kingdom vision also involves:

**Teaching from a Biblical Perspective**

Our age is an age of secularism. The essence of secularism is that it views reality apart from God and claims that life can be lived without God. Secularism is clearly reflected in the well-known words of the Russian cosmonaut Yuri Gagarin who, having circled the earth in April 1961, returned to say, "I looked and looked, but didn't see God."

To prepare for the future in such a context, the Christian teacher must obviously work from a biblical perspective. I'm sure you've heard this before, and perhaps you've wondered what this means for your work as a classroom teacher. I don't intend in this one brief presentation to give an exhaustive response, but it seems that you must have a biblical perspective in at least four areas.

First, Christian teachers must have a biblical view of themselves as restored image-bearers of God. As we've already indicated, they occupy the office of teacher, to which they have been appointed and for which they have been qualified by none other than Christ. Therefore, they must evidence a spirit of humble obedience because they are responsible to Christ. But they can also express an attitude of confidence because they are qualified to represent Christ.

Second, Christian teachers must have a biblical understanding of their task. In the classroom, they are not parents who are called to provide family nurture for their students—although they should be aware of and build on such nurture. They are not clerics who are called to preach to and evangelize the children—although they must be sensitive to and supportive of such efforts. The calling and task of Christian teachers takes place within the school in which their task is to lead their students academically to a greater understanding of the creation, the history of creation, and their place in the creation-kingdom of God.

Third, Christian teachers must have a biblical view of their students. Instead of viewing them as organisms to be manipulated in behavioristic fashion, students must be seen as image-bearing, religious beings who have been made and remade, created and recreated to respond believingly and obediently to the Word of the Lord. In this view, teachers will respect students as image-bearers, direct them as religious beings, and increasingly appeal to their sense of always being responsible *coram deo*, before the face of God.

Fourth, and most importantly, Christian teachers must have a biblical perspective on their subject material. The task of the teacher has been defined as that of leading students to a greater understanding of the creation, its history, and their place in the creation-kingdom of God. This clearly implies understanding what it means to lead students, i.e., pedagogy; knowledge of the creation as reflected in the teacher's particular discipline or aspect of creation; and a perspective on the creation that is integrally normed by the Word of God.

Again, the development of such a biblical perspective on self, task, student, subject—and perhaps more—is the only way to prepare Christian teachers to confront the secularism of our age.

We have in no sense exhausted our topic, but time requires that we conclude our presentation. We do that by noting that in preparing for the future, Christian teachers must:

### Be Gripped by a Sense of Mission

Our age is an age where we are centered on self. We are often called to self-fulfillment, i.e., the discovery of personal talents and the realization of personal potential. When directed by that spirit, our mission and purpose in life is easily focused entirely on self. Preparing teachers for the future in this climate means preparing them to advance, to promote themselves in the world of education; and, for effective teachers, it means preparing students for success as that is defined by the ever-changing norms of contemporary society.

Obviously, we are not opposed to the preparation of effective teachers and the training of successful students. But the Bible calls us to a different mission, to a different purpose, i.e., to "seek first his kingdom and his righteousness" (Matthew 6:33). Christian teachers, to be effective, must be prepared for a kingdom mission where they acknowledge Christ as King, the world as His kingdom, and the subjects being taught as means whereby their students, to be successful, are brought to understand the kingdom and their place and task in it. Does this involve assisting students in discovering and developing their individual gifts and talents? Indeed, it does—but always so that, with those gifts and talents, they may step into their office as part of the Christian community directed by the Word with a sense of mission to seek first the kingdom of God.

Seeking the kingdom of God sounds like reaching into the future, doesn't it? Yes, it is that; but it also involves taking hold of a present reality. As Gordon Spykman notes in the introduction to *Reformational Theology: A New Paradigm for Doing Dogmatics*:

> The kingdom, therefore, now stands as a settled reality securely anchored in God's past acts of salvation ("the kingdom is at hand"), as an abiding, present, coming reality (the redemption "already" in Christ), and as an assured hope based on the promise of a future fully restored reality (the eschatological "not yet" on the way to its consummation). (1992, p. 11)

Preparing Christian teachers for the future means providing them with a sense of mission that inspires them to point students to dedicated service in the "already" and "not yet," in the kingdom of God that has come and is yet to come.

### Conclusion

As we look to the future of our pluralistic, materialistic, individualistic, secular, self-centered society, we can know that Christian teachers, directed by a kingdom perspective, will be prepared to be different as they seek to prepare students for their calling, task, office as qualified and committed citizens of the kingdom of God—prepared to respond positively to the call of the Scriptures:

> Therefore, I urge you, brothers, in view of God's mercy, to offer your bodies as living sacrifices, holy and pleasing to God—this is your spiritual act of worship. Do not conform any longer to the pattern of this world, but be transformed by the renewing of your mind. Then you will be able to test and approve what God's will is—his good, pleasing and perfect will. (Romans 12:1–2)

## References

Schrotenboer, P. G. (1972). *Man in God's world.* Toronto, ON: Wedge Publishing Foundation.

Seerveld, C. ( n.d.). Cultural Objectives for the Christian Teacher. Trinity College, Palos Heights, IL.

Spykman, G. (1992). *Reformational Theology: A new paradigm for doing dogmatics.* Grand Rapids, MI: Eerdmans.

Stronks, G. G. and D. Blomberg, eds. (1993). *A vision with a task: Christian Schooling for responsive discipleship.* Grand Rapids, MI: Baker Books.

# Chapter Twelve

**To the Reader –**

When I was a student at Calvin Theological Seminary, I can remember studying Eschatology, the doctrine of the last things. Included in that study was a consideration of "Millennial Views," specifically premillennialism, postmillennialism, and amillennialism. I recall that I found the study quite interesting, but I'm sure I didn't realize its importance or significance at that time.

Years later, when I was in graduate school, I took a course titled "Sociology of the Future." Each member of the class was assigned at the beginning to write a paper describing his or her view of the future. The assignment for the end of the course was to write a paper indicating how the lectures, readings, and discussions had changed our views of the future. I wrote my beginning paper based on the amillennial position, which has always been the prevalent view in Reformed circles. The professor, who did not profess to be a Christian, responded positively to my paper, indicating that he envied the certainty with which I set forth my beliefs concerning the future. I recalled his comment when, a few months later, he died of a heart attack.

That was 1977. In 1985, I received an invitation to address the 1986 Christian Schools International Convention at Wheaton College in Wheaton, Illinois. The theme of the convention was "Christian Education: Pathway to the Future," and I was asked to address the closing session. By this time I realized the significance of the various millennial views, especially as they related to a biblical understanding of the Kingdom of God. Given that realization, I decided to reflect on these views and their implications for Christian education under the title "Christian Education and the Future of the Kingdom." Following my address, I was encouraged when a Christian school board member said to me, "Thank you for making clear that Reformed theology does have something to say to important issues, such as the Christian education of our children."

# CHRISTIAN EDUCATION AND THE FUTURE OF THE KINGDOM

"Christian Education: Pathway to the Future," has been the theme of this CSI Convention. So, for the past three days, we've been focusing on the future of Christian education—talking about it, thinking about it, singing about it, and praying about it. But, now that we have come to the end of the Convention, whether we like it or not, we must *face* the future.

Some like the idea of facing the future because they are optimistic about the future. The present is great, but the future promises to be even greater. The optimist is eager to face the future. Others cringe at the idea of facing the future because they are pessimistic about the future. The present is terrible, and the future promises to be even worse. The pessimist does not want to face the future. But, again, like it or not, we must face the future.

All of which raises the question: how shall we, as Christian educators, face the future? Much will depend, of course, on the perspective from which we approach the future. We could take the optimistic approach of Herman Kahn and Anthony J. Weiner in their book *The Year 2000*, forecasting a future of worldwide growth and affluence. Or we could take the rather pessimistic approach of The Global 2000 Report to the President of the U.S.A.—a report that has been largely ignored by the president—predicting a world population of six billion by the year 2000, enormous deforestation, increase in deserts, decrease of fresh water supplies, extinction of a half million species of plants and animals, etc. Both viewpoints would obviously impact the future of education.

I'm not suggesting that we ignore these viewpoints; in fact, we intend to give them quite a bit of attention. But on this occasion, given the fact that we are Christian educators inquiring about the future of Christian education, I will focus on the biblical, kingdom approach—also in evaluating these various viewpoints. This approach should appeal to us for several reasons, especially since we're involved in preparing young

---

Closing address delivered at the Christian Schools International (CSI) Convention, Wheaton College, Wheaton, Illinois, August, 1986.

people for kingdom service. In fact, Christian education can be classified as kingdom education preparing young people for further kingdom service. Therefore, as this convention comes to a close, I want to talk to you about Christian education and the future of the Kingdom.

In this presentation I intend to consider three views of the future and, by way of evaluation, to point out the implications of each for Christian education.

**An Optimistic View of the Future**

First, we consider an optimistic view of the future, as set forth by what theologians have called modern postmillennialism—in distinction from the traditional post-millennialism of such as A. H. Strong. Strong wrote that the millennium will be:

> . . . a period in the later days of the Church militant, when, under the special influence of the Holy Spirit, the spirit of the martyrs shall appear again, true religion be greatly quickened and revived, and the members of Christ's churches become so conscious of their strength in Christ that they shall, to an extent unknown before, triumph over the power of evil, both within and without. (1912, p. 1013)

According to the modern postmillennial view, a new age will eventually dawn upon us, but the coming of that age will not be dependent upon God or His Word. Instead, the future of the kingdom is and will be dependent either upon a process of evolution producing an era of peace and prosperity or upon human activity seeking to overcome the ills and evils of our society. The kingdom will come as humanity confronts and conquers disease, poverty, sexism, racism, injustice, and war. The future is bright, but that future depends ultimately upon the noble efforts of humanity.

An optimistic view of the future! But what does such a view mean for education?

It should be obvious that this optimistic view of the future does not require Christian education. To prepare young people for the challenges of the future, depending solely on human intelligence and activity, all that is needed is good education, education of high quality. We've heard much about this lately, i.e., the importance of quality in education for the future of our nation.

A recent article in *Christian Home and School* reported that, according to a number of experts, quality in contemporary high school education requires the following:

- An instructional hour defined as 55 minutes of teaching.

- The instructional hours must be extended to 1140 hours per year.
- Basic skills must be tested in grades 4, 7, and 10.
- Teachers must receive competency testing and certification in their field from teacher training institutions.
- A teacher must be recertified every five years.
- A course must be taught only by a teacher who has a college major or minor in that subject.
- The minimum curriculum mandatory for all students shall be four years of English, three years of mathematics, three years of science, three years of social studies, one-half year of computer science, and for the college-bound students, two years of foreign language are strongly recommended. (1986)

Quality education! This is what is needed for us to make a pathway into the future!

But now, what shall we say to all of this?

First, we cannot accept this optimistic view of the future, because it is fundamentally secular. Indeed, we must work hard to overcome the evils and promote the well-being of our society. Still, while our efforts are used to that end, ultimately their success is not dependent upon human intelligence and activity but rather upon the providential government and preserving activity of our God.

Further, we must reject the view of education promoted by the optimistic view as being essentially non-Christian. Indeed, Christian education must be good education; in fact, we must seek to make it the very best education—and many of the recommendations of the experts will help us to that end. But good, high quality education—as presently described—is not necessarily Christian education and, therefore, does not necessarily prepare for service in the kingdom of Christ.

I want to stress this point, especially in light of the contemporary emphasis upon quality. It is good that we be concerned about "a nation at risk" (Harvey, 1983). It is also important that we promote excellence in education. But let us never get so caught up in this matter of quality that we forget that without Christ even excellent education is inadequate as a pathway into the future.

**A Somber View of the Future**

Next, we consider a somber view of the future as set forth by what theologians have called dispensational premillennialism, in distinction from historical premillennialism. Premillennialism in general is based primarily on a literal method of biblical interpretation. However, L. Berkhof (1949, p. 712) observes that "Premillennarians are by no means all agreed as to the particulars of their eschatological scheme. A study of their literature continues to reveal a great variety of opinions. There is indefiniteness and uncertainty on many points. . . ." What Berkhof has observed about premillennialism in general is also true about dispensational and historical premillennialism. Still a basic difference can be noted between the two, namely, the emphasis that each gives to the nation of Israel during the millennium, the thousand year period during which Christ supposedly will reign on earth.

Historical premillennialism does not require a strict dichotomy between the Church and Israel. It looks ahead to a time when Christ will reign visibly on the earth before He ushers in the eternal state. It holds that the nation of Israel will undergo a national salvation immediately before the millennium is established; but there will not be a national restoration of Israel. Therefore, the nation of Israel will not have a special function that is distinct from the Church.

Dispensational premillennialism has gained popularity among contemporary evangelicals. It was given wide publicity a few years ago with the publication of *The Late Great Planet Earth* (Lindsey, 1970). At this point, because of the limits of time, I must generalize. But, according to this view the Old Testament kingdom of God was limited to the nation of Israel in the land of Palestine. Jesus Christ, the promised Messiah, came to make the kingdom universal by means of His redemptive work. But the Jews refused to receive Him—they rejected and crucified Him. The Messiah, therefore, withdrew in defeat, a King in flight, postponing the coming of His kingdom. As an interim arrangement Christ established His Church.

The second coming of Christ will be preceded by a seven year period of Tribulation—prior to which a secret rapture of the saints will occur. This coming of Christ may occur at any moment. Christ will return to Jerusalem, bringing in His one thousand year kingdom reign. The nation of Israel will be saved and restored to a place of preeminence. The millennium will be a time of Jewish dominion over all the world, including a newly restored Jewish temple and priesthood.

At the conclusion of this one thousand year reign, Satan will be loosed and Gog and Magog will come in revolt against the Holy City. But, Christ will crush this revolt. Gog and Magog will be devoured by fire and Satan will be cast into the pit. The wicked, i.e., those of the world, will be raised, judged, and condemned; and the redeemed, i.e., those of the church, will be settled in the new heavens and the new earth.

In light of this perspective, reality will then be divided into two realms, i.e., the private and the public, the sacred and the secular. The church, worship, doctrine, and issues of morality are all limited to the sacred realm, which is private and points in a vertical direction. Politics, economics, labor, the arts and sciences, and the media are all assigned to the secular realm, which is public and points in an historical direction. Further, because Christ's kingdom has not yet come we must flee the world, the secular realm; we must concern ourselves primarily with the church and evangelism. If we do enter the world of politics, economics, agriculture, and technology, it must be primarily for the sake of witnessing and evangelizing in a world that has rejected and continues to oppose the kingdom of Christ.

A somber view of the future! But what does this view mean for education?

Such a view of the future does call for Christian education, but of a very limited sort. Usually, this perspective insists upon a Christian approach only in courses dealing with the Bible, theology, morality, and values; however, it allows a so-called "neutral" approach to secular subjects.

Actually what the somber view of the future requires is not so much Christian education as church education. If Christian education is to provide a pathway to the future, it must be established and controlled by the church and be based on a church creed; it must seek to evangelize, claiming young people for Christ; and it must prepare young men and women, no matter what their intended vocations may be, to present an evangelizing witness for Christ—calling others out of the devil's world into Christ's church, hoping that soon Christ will come bringing in His kingdom.

But how shall we evaluate this perspective?

To begin with, we have difficulty with this somber view of the future because it is fundamentally dualistic. It errs in that it pictures Christ as a king in flight; it limits Christianity to the realm of the sacred and to the sphere of the church; and, by postponing the coming of the kingdom to an unknown tomorrow, it leaves the rest of the world to the influences of secularism.

Also, we find this view of Christian education troubling because it is far too narrow and limited in its focus. It may prepare young people for service in the church and for life in the vertical dimension; but it has little to say concerning service in the kingdom and for life on the horizontal level.

I also want to stress this point, because I confronted this perspective in my graduate program and increasingly hear comments in the Reformed community that reflect this limited view point.

Parents tell me, "Our son goes to Iowa State, but we're not concerned because during the first semester he came back to his home church to make public confession of faith, and the university football coach tells us that he is a wonderful witness to his faith." It's fine that their son made confession of faith in the church, but how does his faith shape the rest of his life? It's also fine that this young man witnesses in the presence of the coach and football team, but does that justify turning his education over to a system that insists on privatizing his faith and declaring the rest of life neutral?

Back to my graduate program. I attended a theological school regarded as the most liberal in the United Methodist Church community. I enrolled in their program of "Religion and Higher Education," since I was interested in the integration of faith and learning. But, in spite of my description of Christian education as education where "all the students' intellectual, emotional, and imaginative activities shall be permeated with the spirit and teaching of Christianity" (*Scripturally-Oriented Higher Education,* p. 2), it was obvious that the school was thinking only of church education and preparation for church ministry.

In light of a biblical worldview, this perspective just does not wash. And what is more, as Middleton and Walsh, authors of *Transforming Vision* (1984) state, such end-times theology really offers no hope for the future.

## A Reformed View of the Future

Finally, we consider what we believe is a Reformed view of the future, as set forth by what is usually described theologically as amillennialism. In the beginning, God established His kingdom when, by His Word, He created the heavens and the earth and mankind as His image-bearing servants.

God established His kingdom within the context of the covenant, i.e., that agreement between God and His creation whereby, in the service of its Creator, the creation would enjoy the blessings of life. The covenant was to be realized through mankind, called to rule creation as God's serving representative. As Herman Hoeksema explains:

> In this covenant relation Adam was the friend-servant and office-bearer of God in all creation. He was God's co-worker. And this calling of Adam in the state of righteousness is to be understood very concretely and real-

istically. His life is not to be vaporized in our imagination into a sort of mystical enjoyment of sweet communion with the Lord under the tree of life. He had work to do. (1953, p. 128)

Mankind was to work in creation obediently, according to God's law. If mankind lived and worked in harmony with the law, the Word of God, the result would be the blessing of life and joy for the entire creation. But mankind fell into sin, refusing to live and work in and with creation according to God's law. Thus mankind broke covenant with God, refused to serve God, and failed to bring to expression God's kingdom. And, instead of life, the result was death.

But death was not history's last word. God came to mankind with another word, the word of redemption that, according to Edward J. Young "appears in germ form from the very beginning" (1965, p. 372) in the promise of Genesis 3:15. By this promise, God re-established His covenant with mankind and the creation. With Abraham the covenant was formalized. At Sinai God's covenant people were organized as a nation and designated as citizens of God's kingdom, called to serve in the kingdom land of Canaan. To David, God gave the promise that One would come to sit on Israel's throne, who would establish a kingdom universal in its scope and eternal in its duration.

Eventually that One came, Jesus Christ, the Mediator of the covenant and the Ruler to govern His kingdom. Through Christ—His death, resurrection, and ascension—God has reconciled the world to Himself and restored mankind to covenantal fellowship with Himself. With Christ as King, God has reclaimed creation as His kingdom, in which the redeemed are to serve Him according to His Word and unto His praise.

*The kingdom has come!* Christ is King. Creation is His kingdom. The redeemed are to serve Him now, everywhere and in all things—in the church, but also in judicial, economic, political activities—bringing to expression everywhere His kingdom rule. *The kingdom is coming!* Jesus is coming back. When He does, He will complete the redemption of God's covenant people and the creation, presenting to His Father a perfected kingdom—the new heavens and earth—that God may be all in all.

That, according to our Reformed perspective, is the present and future of the kingdom. And what does this mean for Christian education?

Such a kingdom view of the future calls for education that is Christian throughout, Christian from beginning to end. It demands a Christian approach not only for courses in Bible, theology, and morality, but also for other courses such as mathematics, chemistry, history, economics, music, and art.

To prepare students for the future as seen from a Reformed, kingdom perspective requires integrated Christian education. We're talking about educational institutions established and controlled not by the church but by the covenant/kingdom community. We want education based not primarily on an ecclesiastical but upon an educational creed, i.e., a confession that reflects our commitment to Christ in the sphere of education. We want education that seeks first of all not to evangelize, but to nurture and develop covenant youth. A Reformed perspective in education does not ignore the church, ecclesiastical confessions, or evangelism; but its primary focus is the covenant community, an educational creed, and the nurture of covenant youth. A Reformed perspective prepares young people not merely for a witnessing life in the church, but also for a kingdom witness in the school, the home, the court, the hospital, the farm, the office, the art studio, the halls of government, and the marketplace. A Reformed perspective calls for education that qualifies young people to deal with real life, with contemporary issues, such as human rights, the arms race, the economic debate, energy and the environment, the new technology, and the Christian's responsibility in a pluralistic society.

Will God bless such education? Indeed, He will. Listen! All authority has been given unto Me. God! "And surely I will be with you always, to the very end of the age" (Matthew 28:18–20).

## Conclusion

The kingdom has come—everywhere, also in the sphere of education. Christ is not a king in flight. By His death and resurrection, He has conquered sin, Satan, and death. He is seated at the Father's right hand, holding the scepter of universal rule and authority. Therefore, every instructor must bow before Him; every course must be viewed in light of His Word; and every student must be prepared to serve Him, no matter what his or her calling may be—for the kingdom has come.

And the kingdom is coming! This Jesus whom you have seen going into heaven shall in like manner return (Acts 1:11). And when He does, the kingdom will come in its perfection. We will sit at the feet of the Master. He will teach and make all things plain to us. His servants—both teachers and pupils—will serve Him. They will see His face, and His name will be on their foreheads. There will be no more night. They will not need the light of a lamp or the light of the sun, for the Lord God will give them light. And they will reign with Him forever and ever (Revelation 22:4–5).

May our Christian schools, directed by this kingdom vision, provide a clear pathway to that challenging, blessed, and certain future.

**References**

*Christian Home and School.* (Spring, 1986). Grand Rapids, MI: Christian Schools International.

Berkhof, L. (1949). *Systematic Theology.* Grand Rapids, MI: Eerdmans.

Harvey, J. J. (April 1983). *A nation at risk: the imperative for educational reform.* Washington, DC: National Commission for Educational Reform.

Hoeksema, H. (1953). *In the midst of death.* Grand Rapids, MI: Eerdmans.

Lindsey, H. (1970). *The late great planet earth.* Grand Rapids, MI: Zondervan.

Kahn, H. and Weiner, A. J. (1967). *The year 2000.* Washington, DC: The Hudson Institute.

Middleton, J. R. and Walsh, B. (1984). *Transforming Vision.* Downers Grove, IL: InterVarsity Press.

*Scripturally-oriented higher education.* (November, 1967). Sioux Center, IA: Dordt College.

Strong, A. H. (1912). *Systematic theology.* Philadelphia, PA: Griffith and Rowland Press.

*The global 2000 report to the president of the U.S.A.* (1980). Washington, DC: The Council on Environmental Quality and the U.S. Department of State.

Young, E. J. (1965). *An introduction to the Old Testament.* Grand Rapids, MI: Eerdmans.

# EPILOGUE

Early in 2009, Louise and I moved from Sioux Center to Pella, Iowa. Since we are getting older, we wanted to be close to one of our daughters but still be part of the Dordt College community. We miss the close connection with Dordt, but are pleased with and thankful to God for our present living situation.

When we were making arrangements for renting a home in Pella, our landlord welcomed us and said, "We'll be looking forward to a good, strong Christian school sermon." I told him that I was no longer accepting preaching requests, but said that perhaps I could speak at a Christian school rally or anniversary celebration—which I had occasionally done in Pella in the years before.

It wasn't long before I was given that opportunity. In April 2010 I was invited to speak at the Friends of Pella Christian High Banquet in celebration of the school's 70th Anniversary. The title of my presentation was "PCHS: A Kingdom Witness," and I'm using it as an epilogue to the preceding 12 discourses on Christian education, since it sums up my ministry on behalf of the youth of God's covenant.

**Friends of Pella Christian High School**

It's an honor to be invited to speak to supporters of Pella Christian High School, especially in this 70th anniversary year. Having known many of your past and present administrators, teachers, and graduates, I've always held this school in high regard. Pella Christian High is a very good school.

If I'm not mistaken, I last spoke to this group at the end of my first year as the president of Dordt College. It was the spring of 1983, and we met in the gymnasium/auditorium of the former high school building. Shortly after our move from Sioux Center to Pella, my wife and I—along with others of you—watched the demolition of that building. We did so with a measure of regret, because that building held many fond memories for us—memories of meaningful chapels, exciting basketball games, stimulating teacher's conferences, memorable graduations, fruitful recruitment visits, and emotional grandparents' days. But now we rejoice with you in this beautiful new building and auditorium and are pleased to be here with you this evening.

When contacted by the planning committee for this event, I was told simply that I should speak in promotion of Christian education. I immediately said, "Yes," because my life in the church and at the college has been involved very much in the promotion of Christian education. From the very beginning of my ministry, as a product of Christian education, I've been of the conviction that Christian schooling is essential to the well-being of our families, our churches, and the kingdom at large. It works both ways: our schools need the support of families, churches, and communities, while our families, churches, and communities need the support of the Christian schools.

But when I say this, I realize that this conviction is being challenged today. For one thing, support for Christian schooling is decreasing. In the denomination to which many of us belong—the Christian Reformed Church—the percentage of children attending Christian schools has decreased from 41 percent in 1978 to 19 percent in 2007. I know that sounds incredible, and I want to double-check those figures; still, that there is a decrease in Christian school support cannot be denied.

But what concerns me just as much, if not more, is the charge that promoting Christian schools hinders our witness in the world, hinders the work of evangelism. It is claimed that there is a conflict between the gospel we preach—inviting and welcoming people into our fellowship—and the education we promote—which seems to elevate and place us in opposition to others.

I don't believe for a moment that that charge is true. In fact, I believe that it reflects a distorted view either of the gospel we preach, or of the Christian education we promote, or of both. In response I want to begin by considering, first:

**The Gospel We Preach**

What is the gospel? The gospel is good news. The gospel, according to Jesus, is "the good news of the kingdom" (Matthew 4:23).

Indeed, the gospel tells us that Jesus saves, but more than that it tells us that, in the beginning, God **created** the heavens and the earth. When He did so, He brought His kingdom into being as the place over which He is sovereign, which He rules according to His Word, and in which He is to be served. Further, the gospel tells us that our **fall** brought the creation under the curse of sin. Turning us from God to himself, Satan claimed the world as his possession, called the truth of God's Word into question, and enslaved humanity in his service. Finally, the gospel informs us that, in the fullness of time, God sent His Son into the world to perform the work of **redemption.** By His death, resurrection, and ascension, Christ defeated Satan and reclaimed the kingdom. Declaring "All authority has been given unto me in heaven and on earth," Christ directs us by His Word and Spirit, calls us in all things to seek first His kingdom, assures us that He will be with us always, "to the very end of the age" when He will **consummate** all things in the new heavens and earth.

Creation, Fall, Redemption, Consummation – concepts that should be familiar to all of us, especially those who have been blessed to receive a Christian education. This is the gospel that has been entrusted to us, the gospel of the kingdom. This is the gospel by which we have been brought into the kingdom and to which we are to give witness in the time and place in which we live. As we heard Rev. Gary Bekker, director of CRC World Missions, recently state: "In our eagerness to be relevant, let's pray that we never cease being reliable witnesses to the truth about Jesus and the Kingdom of God."

But how are we to do this? First, as individual Christians we are to witness to the truth of the kingdom by the words we speak and by the lives we live. As Paul encouraged the Thessalonians, "Make it your ambition to lead a quiet life, to mind your own business and to work with your hands, just as we told you, so that your daily life may win the respect of outsiders" (1 Thessalonians 4:11, 12).

Further, as churches we are to proclaim the gospel of the kingdom from our pulpits and by way of programs of evangelism in our communities, nation, and world. As the Heidelberg Catechism indicates, we are to confess that the only way to live and die happily is to confess our sins, to acknowledge Christ as our Savior, and to commit ourselves to serve Him as our crucified, risen, and exalted King—even as we pray, "Your kingdom come."

But we also bear witness to the gospel of the kingdom through our Christian schools.

Is that true? Do we bear witness to the gospel through our Christian schools? Indeed, we do. If we don't, we should. Consider with me, secondly:

**The Education We Promote**

Remembering the four elements of the gospel of the kingdom that we noted earlier, we continue now by observing that in our Christian schools we bring the light of God's Word to bear on the entire **creation** and all of its creatures, including humans created in the image of God.

The program of study represents the creation order. And every subject in that curriculum—history, music, biology, mathematics, etc.—is to be viewed in the light of Scripture because, as Calvin stated, we can't truly understand the creation unless we view it through the spectacles of Scripture.

Viewing creation from this perspective enables the Christian school teacher, further, to explain how the **fall** into sin has twisted and distorted the creation and our understanding of the creation order. And it enables that same teacher to point out how God, through the **redemptive** work of Christ, has reclaimed the creation as His kingdom and the redeemed as citizens of that kingdom.

In this way, the Christian school prepares its students for kingdom service, i.e., qualifying them to take that which God formed and sin deformed, in order to reform it according to the Word of God—His Word for the church, but also for agriculture, education, government, medicine, and technology. Thus, the Christian school makes known the gospel of the Kingdom, i.e., that Christ is Lord of all, that He rules all things by His Word and Spirit, and that the redeemed—as preachers, farmers, teachers, legislators, physicians, and engineers—must work to bring His kingdom to expression everywhere, making clear that Christ is all and in all (Colossians 3:11).

Notice that Christian education does not intend to isolate its students from or elevate them above the world, as some claim. Rather, it intends to prepare students to live in the world as citizens of the kingdom of God.

Does Pella Christian High School bear witness to the gospel of the kingdom? I believe it does. Turning to the school's Handbook, we note its "Basis Statement":

> God is the creator of heaven and earth. Therefore, we engage in the study of this world acknowledging his sovereign rule over all things in it.
>
> God is the Savior of the world. Therefore, we seek to discern the corruption of mind and will and the claims of God's renewing and redeeming work.

We also note its "General Aims":

> To bring the student to understand that our world belongs to God.
> To bring the student to appreciate the cultural heritage of civilization.
> To develop in students the abilities which God has invested in them for the advance of his kingdom and the enjoyment of his glory.

Finally, we note its "Mission Related Goals":

*Epilogue*

To prepare students for responsible citizenship in God's kingdom.
To promote covenantal Christian education for all Christian families.

All of this is to be done "in a community in which is demonstrated Christian love, wisdom, and purpose."

But, is Pella Christian High actually realizing these goals? I'm confident that all—including the board, administration, teachers, students, and constituents—would acknowledge that these goals are not being realized with perfection. Still, there is an ongoing effort in that direction. In that connection, I was encouraged to read in the *Reporter* that Pella Christian has been granted "special accreditation," i.e., freedom to alter curriculum in light of purpose, while maintaining standards, in order to continue working toward the realization of its goals.

It's important to consider, finally, Pella Christian's graduates. Obviously, I don't know all of them; but, in part because of my work at Dordt College, I am personally acquainted with Pella Christian graduates who are now involved, as kingdom citizens, not only in church ministry but also in environmental programs, medicine, computer services, education, music, art, and government. In other words, I sincerely believe that Pella Christian is realizing its goals, fulfilling its purpose, and bearing witness to the gospel of the kingdom—the kingdom come and coming.

**Conclusion**

It's nonsense, therefore, to suggest that a school such as Pella Christian High School is a hindrance to evangelism. It is an essential part of our testimony to the world that Christ is King, that the world is His kingdom, and that Christ redeems us and our children so that, as citizens of His Kingdom, we may serve Him in all that we do.

For six years, following retirement from the presidency of Dordt College, I served as the Executive Secretary of the International Association for the Promotion of Christian Higher Education (IAPCHE)—an association of Christian colleges, universities, and theological schools throughout the world. All of them are committed to the kingdom perspective I've been describing this evening. Therefore, I regarded my work with them as that of worldwide "academic evangelism."

Shortly after we moved to Pella, my brother and his wife came from Grand Rapids, Michigan to visit us. Driving from Oskaloosa along Highway 163, they passed the new Christian high school building.

Their first comment when they arrived: "Was that the Christian high school?" "Yes," we said. Did they respond by saying "what a beautiful building"? No, but "What a testimony to the Kingdom of God."

This place and what takes place here is a hindrance only to the kingdom of this world. And, as a witness to the kingdom of God, rather than hesitation and doubts, it deserves our wholehearted support!

And it's in this conviction that I've offered *Christian Education: Issues of the Day*.

www.ingramcontent.com/pod-product-compliance
Lightning Source LLC
Chambersburg PA
CBHW032118090426
42743CB00007B/381